IN THE ARENA OF FAITH

THE DAWN OF WORLD REDEMPTION
A Survey of Historical Revelation in
the Old Testament

THE TRIUMPH OF THE CRUCIFIED
A Survey of Historical Revelation in
the New Testament

FROM ETERNITY TO ETERNITY
An Outline of the Divine Purposes

THE KING OF THE EARTH
The Nobility of Man According to
the Bible and Science

IN THE
ARENA OF FAITH

A CALL TO A CONSECRATED LIFE

By

ERICH SAUER

WM. B. EERDMANS PUBLISHING COMPANY
GRAND RAPIDS   MICHIGAN

First printing, August 1955
Second printing, December 1959
Third printing, November 1963
Fourth printing, October 1966
Fifth printing, June 1971

This Edition is published by arrangement with
The Paternoster Press, London, Eng.

PHOTOLITHOPRINTED BY GRAND RAPIDS BOOK MANUFACTURERS, INC.
GRAND RAPIDS, MICHIGAN
1971

TABLE OF CONTENTS

PREFACE

WHAT we need is revival, a spiritual awakening of God's people, a powerful testimony to the world, a new vision and a fresh experience of the saving and keeping power of Christ through His word and the Holy Spirit.

This experience is possible, for Christ is living today! He is the eternal Victor, the Exalted One, the spring of all life and strength for everyone who puts his trust in Him. Christ never disappoints.

But God grants His free gifts only to faith. Only where there is trust and devotion, will God's fountains be opened. Only upon a life, fully surrendered, will He pour out His abundant blessings.

Where there was failure, He can give restoration. All weakness can be overcome. New joy and hope can fill our hearts.

That is the message of this book. It is at the same time my personal testimony. It differs from my previous books, *The Dawn of World Redemption, The Triumph of the Crucified* and *From Eternity to Eternity* in that those dealt with the *general* lines of development of God's plan of redemption, but this bears testimony chiefly to our *personal* experience of salvation. For the deeds of God are not only around and above us, they should be *in* us at the same time. The general plan of salvation must centre in a personal experience of salvation in the individual.

I am indebted very much to my friends Dr. and Mrs. A. E. Wilder Smith for their very great and most valuable share in the work of translation. Without their keen interest and united efforts this English edition would not have come to pass.

The book was published first in German in 1952. In this English edition there is added a special treatise on "The ancient Greek and Roman Racecourses and the Spiritual Warfare, as compared in the New Testament." We have given this discussion in a more detailed form because the knowledge of these Greek and Roman customs illuminates greatly the figurative language of many New Testament Scriptures which refer to them. At the same time it gives us a clearer understanding of the

7

surroundings and some most important features of the outward conditions of the early Christian church. By elaborating the description of this special side of ancient culture in its relationship to the New Testament, we also hope to render a certain service to such students of Scripture who might want to make use of this book for the preparation of messages in their ministry, and therefore might be glad to have a more detailed view of these ancient customs and their history. Such readers may also value the Greek terms of these institutions as well as the references to certain Greek expressions in the Biblical text that are occasionally given in the book when this seemed helpful for a more exact understanding.

The chapter on the Races has been translated by Mr. G. H. Lang, the translator of my three previous books. To him I wish also to express my sincere thanks.

The book is written in a simple style. It sets out to express its message in a language understandable to all. It is designed as an appeal to heart and mind for new spiritual zeal and devotion, for new confidence and hope. It bases its teachings on the truths of Hebrews 12. Therefore at the head of each chapter is given the relevant quotation from Hebrews 12 so that the word of the Scripture and the meditation thereon may hang closely together, and the reading and understanding of the whole be facilitated.

May the Lord bless the testimony of this book. May He lead us all more and more into a real experience of His blessings. His promises are to all those who in holy earnestness reach out towards the prize, those who lift up their eyes to Him, those who do His commandment. In the arena of faith "let us look unto Jesus."

ERICH SAUER

Wiedenest, Rhineland, Germany.

INTRODUCTION

God's people have heard God's call. For only by this call has a People of God come into being, since "faith cometh by hearing" (Rom. 10: 17). By means of this call God's miraculous dealings with His church began. We cannot think or speak highly enough of the redeemed of the Lord. They are saved and reconciled, freed and blessed (Col. 1: 13, 14; Eph. 1: 3). They are "elect of God, holy and beloved" (Col. 3: 12). They are vessels of His grace, sons of the mighty Father, royal children, citizens of heaven. Even though many imperfections and weaknesses are indeed still present, we may be of good courage and have firm confidence as to the work of the Holy Spirit in His own. We are able to see Christ's image in His followers, yes, we can see Christ Himself in our brother and with all our heart we can rejoice in Him seen in one another. "The saints that are in the earth, they are the excellent, in whom is all my delight" (Psa. 16: 3).

And yet——!

God's people need a new awakening! It is an alarming fact that, in spite of the mighty voice of God in the momentous happenings of recent years, there has been no really great lasting *general* revival, not in a single European country!

Certainly in not a few towns and districts the Spirit of God has been able to work in local movements. The general public has been spoken to with power by the gospel. Christians have been quickened and non-Christians won, triumphant songs of thanks and salvation have been heard in churches and tents, in halls and homes. For all these works of grace in town and country we cannot sufficiently bless the Lord.

And yet, amongst believers, we see so much earthly-mindedness, so much love of the world, so much anxiety, so much narrow egoism, so much exclusive concern for one's own little circle, so much firm holding fast to old forms which have long since been dead and which, not seldom, never had any solid warrant in Scripture, so much over-emphasis on secondary matters, and so much neglect of the true values that really matter.

9

We must seriously ask ourselves the question: Have our ears become so deaf that we are not able to hear the voice of God for the thunder of the battlefields, the roaring of the bombers, the crashing of walls, the collapsing of houses, the dying of millions of men and women, old and young?

Without a doubt, *sin* has been at work here. Not God but the demoniacal powers of world kingdoms separated from Him have caused all this. But in this thunder of catastrophies *God* has spoken, secretly controlling them and, in the last analysis, mightily ruling by them (*cf.* Jer. 51: 20; Isa. 45: 1–7): "Come, behold the works of the *Lord*, what desolations *He* has made in the earth" (Psa. 46: 8).

How could God speak yet *more* impressively? First-class world powers have been smashed, towns have been changed to fields of ruins, irreplaceable works of art, centuries old, have been destroyed, millions of men have been killed. Under the judgment of God the estrangement of sinners from Him has worked itself out in a most terrifying manner to their own disaster.

How clearly ought God's people to have recognized God's voice in the midst of this Satan-driven whirl of history! To what a large extent should there have been power-filled witness, missionary energy, readiness to sacrifice, zeal to be sanctified, and willingness to show brotherly love, showing forth thus the fact and the fruit of really living for eternity!

And yet in general one has seen so very little of all this.

How can we expect non-Christians to awake if we ourselves are not awakened? How can "fire" arise if we ourselves do not "burn"? How shall life be begotten if we ourselves are not truly filled with "life"?

Things must be altered. God's people must awake. *You* must awake and 1 .... W- ---+ let ourselves be clothed anew by life-giving power from on high. The living Christ must become again the reality of our souls and take possession of all we are and have.

We must forsake all false quietism and reach out into a holy activity. We must learn anew to regard our Christian life as a "race," as a running (I Cor. 9: 24), as "combat" in the "arena of faith" (*cf.* Phil. 3: 14; Heb. 12: 14). "I therefore so *run*" (I Cor. 9: 26). "Neither count I my life dear unto myself, so that I might finish my *course* with joy" (Acts 20: 24; II Tim. 4: 7), "that I have not *run* in vain" (Phil. 2: 16).

"The prize" is waiting to be won (I Cor. 9: 24). "I press

toward the mark for the prize of the high calling of God in Christ Jesus" (Phil. 3: 14).

"Know ye not that they which run in a race run all, but one receiveth the prize? So run, that ye may obtain" (I Cor. 9: 24).

But he alone has the victory who looks to Christ. For Christ also was a warrior. He was both pioneer and victor. For this reason He is also our example and source of power, our umpire and rewarder.

What we need is a renewed vision of the person of the Redeemer, a vision of the cross and a practical obedience to the ways of the cross, a thankful recognition of God's grace abundantly bestowing its blessings upon us. We must be taken hold of and flooded through and through by the power of His Spirit so that we may run in His strength unto the goal of our calling.

This implies in detail that we must stand the test in difficulties, in sorrows, we must be able to dismiss the spirit of worrying and overcome all spiritual weariness and symptoms of fatigue, we must be ready to bear witness and must have a missionary spirit. Brotherly love and sanctification, prayerfulness and hearkening to the Word of God, must characterize us. All this will enable us to run steadfastly towards heaven and glory.

Such is the purpose of this book. In the main, this is the message of the 12th chapter of the Letter to the Hebrews. And thus the message of God in those bygone days will become a message of admonition and warning for us today, a message of revival from the past for the people of God in the present.

It is these truths that I feel of the greatest importance. In fact, in them lies the fulcrum, the secret of our own intimate heart relationship to the Lord: that is, in personal experience of the crucified and resurrected Christ, in faith in a present full salvation, in the realization of the heavenly standing of the redeemed, in the spirit of joyful gratitude for the richness of blessing which we have received in Christ by the Holy Spirit.

On the other hand we must not fail to confess our very great imperfections. We must see our obligation to strive for practical holiness, the necessity for sacrificial readiness in vital missionary testimony, for steadfast standing of the test in all the trials of the present time. There must be intercourse with the Lord through prayer and through His Word, devotion and dedication, freshness in faith and pressing forward to the goal, realization of responsibility, holy earnestness, and, at the same time, joyful expectancy of His glorious coming again.

All this is possible only through Him, who is Himself the fountain of all salvation. "From Me is thy fruit found" (Hos. 14: 8). "Jesus Christ is the same yesterday, and today, yea and for ever" (Heb. 13: 8). Only an actual God working in the actual experience of man can help us; there must be faith for a realized experience of His person, a reckoning upon His presence. He is at hand (Phil. 4: 5). He is here where I am. His presence is my salvation. He is the ever-ready helper at any moment in my own personal experience and He helps in every situation joyfully, the present living Christ here and now. "Jesus saves me now."

CHAPTER I

"LOOKING UNTO JESUS"

"THE greatest joy in life is to make Jesus Christ known."
I read this in large letters on the wall of the Moody Hall
in Chicago. This word of that great evangelist expresses
the essence of his life and the joy received thereby. These
words should also be the motto of the service and the
striving of all the truly redeemed. We all live "by" Christ.
We all strive "toward" Christ. We all wish to be "in" Him and
"for" Him. Our life is only of as much value as Christ is in us.
Anything that is superadded besides Jesus is worthless. It is
true, the earthly and outward has its value which is not to be
underestimated in this present life, if it is kept within bounds.
We are far from regarding the wonders of creation as of little
import, or giving ourselves over to cynicism or escapism in that
we despise everything that is natural. But we must insist that
only that will remain for our everlasting existence which is today
directed towards Christ in us. Only that has eternal value which
has been lived for Him and loved for Him, which we have done
in Him, which we have suffered for and gained with Him. Jesus
and Jesus alone is *the* life of our life, the eternity of our time, the
value which can never be stolen, ruined or devaluated. For this
reason everything depends on a practical attitude of living faith
to Jesus Christ.

This is the fundamental esseince of all NewTestament spiritual
life. To show forth and practise the truth and the life of Christ
is the content and message of the whole New Testament. Jesus
Christ is for all the New Testament writers the living and only
panacea for all illness, weakness, and distress. Every one of
them is perfectly sure of it: *Jesus never disappoints: Jesus only
wonderfully surprises.* He never does less than He promised. On
the contrary, He exceeds His own word, so that everyone who
really trusts in Him can join in the happy exclamation of the
Queen of Sheba: "Not the half had been told me."

It is not a rhetorical phrase but my most serious conviction when I state: If anyone were to offer me a ball of gold as big as the sun, that is a ball more than one million two hundred thousand times greater than our whole earth—all pure gold—saying, however, at the same time, "You must exchange your faith in the Lord Jesus for this," I should not have to hesitate for one moment. There can be only one answer: "Away with your golden ball into outer space. I despise it. Jesus is of infinitely greater value to me." And I know that I should not be the only one to give this reply. Every real disciple of Christ would give the same answer. Every true believer would so reply, just as promptly, without any hesitation. All created lights of this world are eclipsed to the man for whom Jesus Christ is risen as the sun of righteousness. "A greater than all is here!"

The whole New Testament speaks of this "greater one," of Him who is indeed the greatest of all. For this reason the central message of the whole book is the call: "Let us look unto Jesus!"

Three New Testament writings out of a total of 27 books form a special constellation in this sense: the Gospel of John, the Colossian letter and that to the Hebrews.

In John's Gospel the glory of Christ is radiated as seen from *above*. He is the Son who came down from heaven into this world. He was sent from the Father. Thus we see Christ as viewed under the aspect of heaven. This is *salvation's basis*.

In the Colossian letter we view the glory of Jesus from *within*, *i.e.*, from within Himself, as the living, active Saviour and Redeemer, because of the exceeding greatness of His person (especially in ch. 1), and the all-inclusive sufficiency of His work (especially in ch. 2). Thus we see Christ as viewed under the aspect of His own person and His own work. This is *salvation's centre*.

The letter to the Hebrews shows us the glory of Christ compared with *earlier* times, *i.e.*, the times of the preparation for salvation in Old Testament history. So Christ is here shown as the One Who not only fulfilled God's greatest revelations but infinitely exceeded them (especially in chs. 1–10). Thus we see Christ as viewed under the aspect of preparation and fulfilment. This is *salvation's history*.

Therefore, while the call, "Let us look unto Jesus!" is the motto of the New Testament in general, how much more is it the motto in this radiant constellation of these three Spirit-given Divine messages!

This message, as indeed the message of the whole New Testament, aims at life and reality. "Looking unto Jesus" must justify itself in practice. The message is not concerned with "enthusiasm for Christ" but with being "filled with the Spirit of Christ," not with mere admiration of His greatness, but with practical experience of His all-sufficiency in the trials and tribulations of this everyday life of ours; not only intellectual, spiritual vision, but spiritual action; not only songs of triumph, but a real practical victory; not only worship, but discipleship. Both aspects belong inseparably together: the sanctuary and everyday life, heaven and earth, the exalted Christ and His sanctifying practical life-power to be experienced here below.

The twelfth chapter of the letter to the Hebrews is that portion of the New Testament in which this relationship between the vision of Christ and victory in battle is especially emphasized. We shall consider this chapter from the following chief points of view:

> Let us look unto Jesus!
> For He is our *example in conflict*.   Verses 1–3.
> Let us look unto Jesus!
> For thus we can *attain practical victory*.   Verses 1–3.
> Let us look unto Jesus!
> For thus we *remain steadfast in suffering*.   Verses 4–11.
> Let us look unto Jesus!
> For thus we shall *not become weary in the race*.   Verses 12–15.
> Let us look unto Jesus!
> For thus we can *live up to the privileges of our birthright*.
> Verses 16–17.
> Let us look unto Jesus!
> For thus we shall *attain unto the crown and the heavenly City*.
> Verses 18–29.

This looking *unto* Jesus is at the same time a looking *away* from everything else. For this reason a word is used for "looking" in Hebrews 12 which includes both these meanings.[1] It means a purposeful looking *away* from those objects which automatically catch the eye, *to* those other objects which have to be concentrated upon. By this means all lack of concentration will

---

[1] Greek *ap-horan* from the Greek *apo* = from, away from and *horan* = to look. Cf. Greek *apo-blepein*, Heb. 11: 26.

be overcome. Our eyes will be directed on one object, Christ, and the heart will thereby be held by His glory. Thus the whole inward man experiences in ever-increasing measure the depths and the riches of the Scripture: "They saw no one but Jesus only."

All the blessings of God are so devised that they can increase. That is, every fulfilment is at the same time a promise of something greater. God never reaches the end of His possibilities (John 1: 16; Eph. 2: 7). Thus the best and most glorious is ever before us and to come. All is of glory, in glory, and, according to His own plan, "from glory to glory" (cf. II Cor. 3: 18).

With the world and sin it is otherwise. It starts with mock joy and ends with disappointment. At the beginning there is a deceptive glitter and at the end night.

Many years ago I visited a Press Exhibition in Cologne. In one of the large halls the relationship between the Press and the postal services was shown by various documents and tables. I shall never forget the decoration on one of the main walls. It represented a huge eagle. The exhibition concerned itself with the attainments of the German postal services up to 1928. The effect of this huge eagle was most imposing. But when one came nearer to it and looked at it more closely one discovered that it consisted solely of postage stamps of the inflation period— hundreds of thousands of small inflation postage stamps. I said to my companion immediately: "For estimating things earthly is not this a picture of the values of this world in general? Regarded from a distance, at first sight, they seem to be grand and imposing. But the nearer one comes to them, the more one discovers that they are all inflated values—huge numbers but little worth. Not only inflation of money but inflation of words, inflation of terms, inflation of ideals, inflation of spirit. Behind this mighty façade only very little actual substance. The more one gets to know them the less one values them. From the distance like an eagle, yet in reality only inflation!"

How different is Jesus Christ! His worth for us increases the more we get to know Him. He proves Himself true even in the severest testing of everyday practice. He faileth never. For this reason our whole thought and endeavour should be directed towards Him. He leads us "from faith to faith" (Rom. 1: 17), "from strength to strength" (Psa. 84: 7), "from glory to glory" (II Cor. 3: 18). In Him there is opened an inexhaustible fountain of salvation (Isa. 12: 3; Zech. 13: 1).

Yet we experience this increase in heavenly blessings only when our souls strive forward. Only those who are hungry get satisfied, only those who are thirsty are refreshed (Matt. 5: 6), only those who take their discipleship to be a "race" attain the "prize" of their calling (Phil. 3: 14; II Pet. 1: 10).

Therefore "let us look unto Jesus!" Only so can we be winners and reach in the arena of faith the goal of everlasting glory (Heb. 12: 1-3).

CHAPTER II

CHRIST—THE EXAMPLE IN THE RACE

"Looking unto Jesus the author and perfecter of faith; who for the joy that was set before him endured the cross, despising shame, and hath sat down at the right hand of the throne of God. For consider him that hath endured such gainsaying of sinners against himself, that ye wax not weary, fainting in your souls." (Hebrews 12: 2, 3.)

ALL depends on how one looks at life. He who would live aright, must see aright. He who would live aright as a Christian, must look upon Christ. "If you wish to be disappointed, look upon others. If you wish to be downhearted, look at yourself. But if you wish to be encouraged and to experience victory, look upon Jesus Christ." He, Jesus alone, is the source of power for all who run in the arena of faith and who would reach the goal of their calling.

The writer of the letter to the Hebrews shows us in chapter 12 a magnificent picture of the Crucified One. Christ endured the cross. Without this central event in the history of revelation there would be no salvation. For this purpose the message of Christ and His sacrificial death, in connexion with the triumph of His resurrection, must occupy the central place in the foreground of all true and Scriptural and effective preaching of the gospel.

In the arena of faith:

"Let us look unto Jesus!" He endured the cross:

1. *As the steadfast Hero with an unflinching will to attain unto victory.*

What outwardly appeared to be weakness was in fact inward power and strength. How easy it would have been for Him to have come down from the cross and freed Himself. Without any difficulty He could have prayed the Father for "twelve legions of angels," which surely would have been granted Him (Matt.

26: 53). We can hardly imagine what that would have meant. When God in the days of Hezekiah saved Jerusalem which was attacked and much oppressed by the Assyrians, He sent only one angel out against this strong military might of the Assyrians, and this *one* angel destroyed one hundred and eighty-five thousand Assyrian soldiers and officers in one night (II Kings 19, 35). Now Jesus declares that, had He only wished it, whole legions of angels would have come to His aid to destroy His enemies. The word "legion" is taken from Roman military use. The Roman legion, on a war footing, consisted of 6,000 soldiers. So this would mean, if we express ourselves in modern military terms, that heavenly armies to the order of brigades and divisions would have come to His aid. And only a single member of these ten thousands of heavenly warriors could have destroyed in one single night hundreds of thousands of His enemies!

If only Christ had wished it! But He did *not* wish it. He knew that the vicarious redemptive sacrifice could be offered only by holding firmly on His way of suffering and so bringing redemption to the world. And therefore He remained on the way of suffering. Therefore He held out until the goal was reached and until in the hour of death on Golgotha He could cry victoriously, "It is finished!" (John 19: 30).

The Hebrews letter most strongly emphasizes this steadfastness and unflinching will to conquer on the part of Jesus. This amazing situation on Golgotha is described in three steps:

He, the Lord of the Universe, endured "contradiction" of earth-born creatures, indeed "great" contradiction, yes, even "so" great contradiction.

He, the King of Glory, allowed Himself to be despised and put to shame, and then, in the midst of all this shame, in true kingly dignity, He "despised the shame." And finally:

He, the Perfect and Holy One, endured all this at the hands of "sinners." Sinners treated Him thus. Sin is in reality the dishonouring of the creature. That means that creatures who had lost their own honour through sin robbed Him, the holy King of glory, of His honour. They even expelled Him from human society by executing Him as a criminal, as they regarded Him.

To bear all this without being compelled to do so; to make no use of all the power which could have helped; to allow oneself to be conquered when one is in reality vastly superior to one's enemies, and all this only in order to reach a high goal—this is indeed unflinching will to conquer, unequalled steadfastness, this is real genuine heroism of indescribable, unrivalled greatness. Of a truth, Christ, the greatest of all endurers, was the greatest hero-warrior just in this, His enduring.

In the arena of faith:

"Let us look unto Jesus!" He endured the cross:

2. As Leader and perfect Exponent of the faith.

Christ is the "Author and Perfecter of faith." Scripture does not speak here only of "our" faith in the sense that Christ is the creative basis of our personal faith through His sacrificial death, His resurrection, and the preaching of the gospel through the Holy Ghost, or in the sense that He keeps us in the faith, perfects our faith and brings His own people to the goal. The Scripture here speaks of faith *in general*. The same word (Gk. *archegos*), which is translated in Hebrews 12 by the English word "author," occurs in Hebrews 2: 10, where it is translated "captain," *i.e.*, leader of an army of faith. The Object of our faith had Himself practised faith. This, in the sense of "trusting," He did even before His incarnation, indeed, before the creation of the world, in an eternal Divine manner. For there can never have been a moment when the Son did not trust the Father. Thus He *originated* the principle of faith (trust) in God, "and He *perfected* the development and display of faith by surrendering His original glory, by stepping down to the state of manhood, by walking on earth as a dependent being and above all by surrendering Himself unto the death of the cross" (G. H. Lang). "Inasmuch as the Son must have from eternity trusted the Father, He was the first to have exercised faith, and so is its Author. On the cross He brought faith to its highest conceivable development, and so became its Perfecter."

Thus He, as pioneer of faith, goes before His own, showing them the way by Himself believing, and thus His faith becomes the most perfect example of faith. The true Son of God and of man showed in Himself how faith may be raised to the highest degree of perfection. Jesus showed perfect faith. In this way He is at once Author, Pioneer, Forerunner, full Exponent and Perfecter of faith.

This is most wonderfully shown in His cry of victory: "It is finished!" If this cry had been uttered on the resurrection morning or after the ascension to the throne of God's glory, one would perhaps have understood it—we say this in all reverence. But Christ uttered this cry at Golgotha, at the very moment of apparent defeat, when the sun had been darkened, when bodily and spiritual sufferings were at the worst, when His enemies mocked Him and triumphed over Him, when the dark moment of death was approaching ever nearer, *then* He cried: "It is finished!" In the darkest hour of the history of the whole world He gave utterance to the most radiant cry of victory ever heard in earthly or supernatural history. If in fact faith is, according to the testimony of the Hebrews letter, the "substance" (realization) of things "hoped for," the "evidence" (conviction) of things "not seen" (Heb. 11: 1), then the faith described here as exercised by Jesus·is of the most perfect order. Never has anyone so exercised faith as Jesus on Golgotha. Faith was brought here to a state of absolute perfection. For this very reason Christ is the One, who, enduring the cross, became not only the Pioneer and Captain of faith, but in the deepest meaning of the word the Perfecter of faith. In Him we see for the first time what true faith actually is.

At the same time the perfect *humanity* of the incarnate Son of God shines before our eyes (John 1: 14).

It is our habit, and rightly so, to regard the deity of the Redeemer and His eternal relationship as Son of God as the central point in our spiritual thinking. Of a truth, Jesus of Nazareth, who made His pilgrim way through this world and then was crucified for our sakes on the cross, was "God manifested in flesh" (I Tim. 3: 16), "God blessed for ever" (Rom. 9: 5). But we should never forget that He was God revealed "in *flesh*," that is, truly as a man in life and nature. Or as one of the early church fathers expressed himself: "He remained what He was. He became what we are." "He was at once in *His* own world and nature as equally in *our* own world and nature." To try to clear up this mystery would be foolishness. The mystery of His incarnation is for ever unfathomable. Christ did not only *work* miracles, He *was himself* a miracle, He is *the* miracle of *all* miracles, the original archetypical miracle. We must recognize the truth of His humanity and the truth of His deity. In Christ we have a man on this earth who perfectly carried out the will of God. In Him it became clear what God meant when He said: "Let us make man in our image, after our likeness" (Gen. 1: 26). Christ's life on earth is the perfect explanation of the meaning of the creation of man.

How encouraging and refreshing it is to know that this perfect Man has given us the proof that it is possible to live in faith here on earth, in our present circumstances, in such a way as perfectly to glorify God.   When we look at His heavenly priesthood from this point of view, how effective and vital it becomes.   "For we have not an high priest which cannot be touched with the feeling of our infirmities; but was in all points tempted like as we are, yet without sin" (Heb. 4: 15).

For this reason meditation on the humanity of the Incarnate One is not a speculative problem of Christian theological philo- sophy, but a subject for serious contemplative thought for the believing heart, so that it may be encouraged to go on in the way of practical sanctification.   Our Lord's example is given to form and educate us.   The picture of Jesus given us in the Gospels should not be used exclusively for evangelistic purposes, that is, chiefly for those who are "without" in order to win their souls; it should be used just as much for ourselves to teach us practical faith in life and sanctification.   This applies both for the regular devotional Scripture readings of the individual and for public ministry in the church.

The true humanity of the Redeemer and His life of faith on earth give us the reason why the author of the letter to the Hebrews does not introduce Him in our verse by His title as "Christ"; he does not say, "Let us look unto Christ," but he names Him by His name "Jesus" to emphasize His humanity and does not even add the word "Christ," or any title belonging to His deity, such as "*Kyrios*" (= "Lord"').   He says quite simply: "Let us look unto *Jesus*."   This is done purposely, just as in other parts of the New Testament the two names "Jesus" and "Christ" are carefully distinguished.

"Jesus" is the name which was given to the Son at His incar- nation (Matt. 1: 21).   This name is therefore connected in a special manner with the period of His life on earth, His true humanity and His humiliation.   It is the name which He has in common with other men (*e.g.,* Jesus Sirach, Jesus Justus: Col. 4: 11).

"Christ" is His title as Messiah, into the full meaning of which He entered later by His ascension and exaltation.   "Therefore let all the house of Israel know assuredly, that God has made that same Jesus, whom ye have crucified, both Lord and *Christ*" (Acts 2: 36).

Thus the reason is clear why the Gospels speak mostly of

"Jesus" while the Epistles use mostly the title "Christ." For the Gospels treat mostly of the time of His humiliation, while the Epistles testify of Him as the raised and exalted One. It is only in the places in the Epistles where the past humiliation of the Incarnate One is emphasized that the name "Jesus" appears alone (II Cor. 4: 10; Phil. 2: 10; I Thess. 4: 14; Heb. 2: 9; 13: 12). The passage which we are now considering also treats of the time of humiliation of the true Son of Man, and thus the use of the name "Jesus" here shows again how perfect and exact is the inspired Word of God.

In the arena of faith:

"Let us look unto Jesus!" He endured the cross:

3. *As triumphal Victor in unwavering hope.*

"For the joy that was set before him" He took upon Himself the suffering. What was this joy? Not the glory of the *Logos* which He had as the everlasting "Word" before His incarnation; not the joy in the world, which the Tempter would have given Him if He had only taken all the glory of the kingdoms of this world out of his hand, instead of going the way of the cross (Matt. 4: 8–10); not even the simple joy in mere freedom from earthly human sufferings in general which He could have had, had He only avoided the cross; but the *future* joy is meant which Christ beheld ever before Him: the completed redemption, the *Ekklesia* which one day should be won, the glorifying of the Father, His own personal position as Victor in the glory after a completed work—in fact just the joy which He would have if He held out steadfastly right on to the end.

In the statement, "He endured the cross *for* the joy that was set before Him," the Greek word *anti*, just as its English equivalent "for," could indeed also mean "instead of," so as to mean that Christ had the choice between the enjoyment of heavenly or earthly blessings on the one hand and humiliation unto the death of the cross on the other hand, and that he endured the cross "instead" of this joy. But in our connexion the word must have its other meaning "in order to"—"in order to" bring in something valuable for which one must do or endure something, "in order to" gain or attain it; Christ endured the cross "*in order to* attain the joy which lay before Him." The word *anti* is used here with the same meaning as in Hebrews 12: 16, where it says that Esau sold his birthright *in order to* attain the pottage. The

decisive factor, however, that *anti* means here "in order to" is
the context, which in the symbol of the race speaks of the athlete
keeping the eye set wholly on the reward, and at the same time
places the word "set before Him" (Gk. *prokeimenos*) in connexion with the word "joy." One must also remark that this
Greek word *prokeimenos* for "set before" is often used with
respect to public gifts intended to honour a person. These gifts
were used as prizes in the Greek races and were publicly exhibited, *i.e.*, "set before" the eyes of all onlookers. Professor
A. Tholuck, the well-known German theologian, calls this word
prokeimenos even the "technical term" for such rewards when
these were exhibited as prizes before the races to those who took
part in them.

So Jesus in His "race" looked steadfastly upon the coming
joy. He did not allow Himself to be turned aside from the future
to anything connected with the present. His suffering took place
in the anticipation of joy. His faith as He was adorned with the
crown of thorns was at the same time a sure hope of the kingly
crown of heavenly glory.

And God gave His approval to this attitude of faith and hope
in the Crucified One. Therefore we see Jesus, who was made a
little lower than the angels, crowned with glory and honour for
the very reason that He suffered unto death. The words in
Hebrews 2: 9, "for the suffering of death" refer to "crowned"
and not to "made a little lower." The text here does not mean
that Jesus was made a little lower than the angels in order to be
able to die, as the King James Version takes it, but that He was
exalted "because" He had been willing to die, as the Revised
Version rightly translates: "crowned because of the suffering of
death." The text does not speak of the incarnation but of the
ascension. The thought is the same as that behind Phil. 2: 9:
"*Wherefore* [because of His obedience unto the death of the cross]
God also has highly exalted Him." Christ's way went through
humiliation to glorification, through rejection to recognition,
from cross to crown. His self-humbling is the reason why He
is now "in the midst of the throne," in the glory as the "Lamb
as it had been slain," bearing the marks of the wounds of His
love (Rev. 5: 6). And for this same reason the "new song" is
sung there: "Thou art worthy to take the book and to open the
seals thereof [the book of the consummation of God's ways of
redemption with mankind and the earth], for thou wast slain and
hast redeemed unto God by thy blood men of every tribe, and

tongue, and people, and nation; and madest them unto our God
a kingdom and priests: and they shall reign upon the earth"
(Rev. 5: 9–10).   Jesus as the Lamb of God is, by the glory of the
Father, the highly exalted and triumphant Perfecter of the world.

When Paul speaks of this exaltation of the One Who was
formerly humiliated, he feels that it is almost impossible to find
a word which expresses the full measure of *this* exaltation and
glorification.   As is so often the case, he is confronted here with
the fact that the otherwise so rich and manifold Greek language
does not possess a word adequate to express that which must
be expressed here.   The fact is that the language of men does
not possess a suitable word simply because human experience does
not rise to the matter to be expressed.   So Paul invents a *new*
word and says that God did not simply "exalt" or "highly
exalt" Jesus, but that He "super-exalted" Him (Gk. *hyper-
hypsosen*).   All other exaltation is nothing compared to *His*
exaltation.   All mountains are but plains compared with the
summit of *this* high mountain range to which God has "hyper-
exalted" Jesus.   Compared to His greatness all other greatness
is a sheer nothing.   This is the answer of God to the unflinching
faith and hope of the Crucified One.

But all these words are found in the Scriptures in order to
serve a practical end.   When we are exhorted to look unto Jesus,
and when He is presented to our eyes in this connexion in His
heroic steadfastness, His perfect faith, and His purposeful hope,
all this is written in God's Word to encourage us to genuine,
actual discipleship in life and practice.

Christ endured the cross:

4. *As the Example that should encourage and empower His followers.*

The purpose of the exhortation "Let us look unto Jesus!" is,
in the context of the letter to the Hebrews: Let us, looking unto
Jesus, gain courage to follow after Him in the arena of faith.
The look unto the Crucified One gives us new courage in every
situation.   Even suffering is brought by the cross into its right
perspective.   In order to weigh up our own difficulties aright we
must consider what Jesus suffered and think over what a contradiction of sinners He endured.   That is the encouragement
which arises out of looking unto Jesus.   The exact meaning of
the Greek word for "consider" (*analogizesthai*) is "to reckon, to

count the cost, to check a calculation, to calculate carefully." It occurs *e.g.,* III Macc. 7: 7; I Clem. 38: 3. So we have to "calculate" what Jesus suffered, and just as He was unflinching we also would be unflinching. He exercised faith, therefore let us also live in faith. He hoped while suffering and looked onward to the crown; so let us also keep our eyes fixed on the goal. Christ, the Crucified One, is not only our Saviour but also our Example. We are not intended merely to cast a glance after Him but to follow after Him. We are not only to meditate upon Him, but we must respond to Him; not only to admire Him, but to obey and in practice to respect Him. Let us not forget: The cross brings not only redemption but also obligation, it not only frees us but binds us, it not only looses us from our former sins but takes possession of us in order to make possible a new, holy life. One cannot in truth believe on the Crucified One without at the same time making His experience on the cross the principle of one's own life and behaviour. "For to this end Christ died and lived again that He might be Lord of both the dead and the living" (Rom. 14: 9). To forsake all (Luke 14: 33), to take up one's cross (Matt. 16: 24), to love Jesus more than the dearest on earth (Matt. 10: 37), to serve Him alone (Luke 16: 13), to hate oneself (Luke 14: 26), to lose one's life so as to gain it for ever (John 12: 25)—this is the attitude of mind which the Crucified One demands of His own. Only this attitude brings the real fellowship of the cross with Him. Only thus is it also possible to live a happy life of fellowship with Him as the Risen One (Rom. 6: 1–14).

During my travels I have often visited places well known through the life of Martin Luther. In fact, I have visited most of them: Eisleben, where he was born and died; Eisenach, where he went to school and studied the classics; Erfurt, where he visited the university and then later in the monastery cell sought a merciful God with many a sigh and a tear; Wittenberg, where he was Professor and where he nailed up his Theses and burnt the Bull of his excommunication by the Pope; Wartburg, where he translated the New Testament; Worms, where he confessed his good confession before the Emperor and the Imperial Diet; Marburg, Coburg, and Halle. In most of these places one sees the so-called "Luther-Rose" on the doors and walls of these houses or in the collections of the letters and documents of the great Reformer.

This rose represents Luther's coat of arms and was designed

by himself. By means of this rose Luther wished to express the main principles of his own faith and of his personal experience of salvation. It is the "symbol of my theology," he once said. In the centre is a black cross in the midst of a red heart, and the whole is surrounded by a white rose on a blue background, surrounded by a golden ring. With this form of seal Luther wished to express symbolically in form and colour what he once wrote in a letter to Lazarus Spengler, the clerk of the city of Nuremberg. It was written on the 8th of July, 1530, during his stay in the castle of Coburg, at the time of the Augsburg Diet: "The first must be a cross, black in the heart, so that I remind myself that faith in the Crucified One saves me. For if we believe in our hearts, we are justified. Even though it is a black cross and mortifies and hurts, yet it leaves the heart in its natural colour (red). It does not destroy our natural personality. It does not kill, but it rather allows us to live. For the just *lives* by faith. This heart must be set in the midst of a white, gay rose, in order to show that faith produces happiness, comfort, and peace, and not as the world gives. For this reason the rose must be white and not red. For white is the colour of the spirits and all angels. This rose is set in the centre of an azure background in order to show that this joy is the beginning of a future heavenly joy. And this background is set in a golden ring in order to show that this blessedness in heaven is everlasting and will never end, and is more precious than all joy and earthly possessions, just as gold is the most precious of all metals." On another occasion Luther expressed himself on the same subject as follows:

> On roses walks the Christian heart,
> E'en though the cross be here its part.

Holy joy, heavenly nature, and everlasting glory is our blessed lot where faith in the Crucified One is the true possession of our heart and the centre of our life. The cross is not a symbol of destruction but of life. It is inextricably connected in Scripture with the resurrection. For Christ's death is at once the death of our death and therefore life and eternal bliss. "Let us look unto Jesus." In the cross is our salvation.

But if Jesus is to be your example, He, the Crucified One, must first have become your Saviour. Before the cross can be our sanctification we must have experienced it as our justification. Before the "new" can begin the "old" must disappear.

Some years ago an artist painted a remarkable, highly symbolical picture. It showed a spitting mouth, a flaming eye, a clenched fist, and—nothing else: No representation of Christ's person—not even any other fully represented human figure. Under this picture are the words: "Prophesy unto us, O Christ, who it was that struck thee?"

The meaning of this picture is plain. It says to us: All you who regard Me, fill in the parts of this picture which are lacking with yourself. *You* are the one who struck Christ. This spitting mouth is *your* mouth. This flaming eye is *your* eye. This clenched fist is *your* fist. You are the one who brought Christ into this, His deep suffering. Do not look around yourself, but look into yourself. Strike your own breast, and confess in humility and shame:

> O sacred Head, what glory,
> What bliss till now was Thine!
> Yet, though despised and gory,
> I joy to call Thee mine:
> Thy grief and Thy compassion
> Were all for sinners' gain;
> Mine, mine was the transgression,
> But Thine the deadly pain.
>
> *Bernard of Clairvaux,* 12th century A.D.
> (translated by *I. W. Alexander*).

How marvellous and all-inclusive is the redemptive power of the Crucified One! Our sins were innumerable. How unfathomable our guilt! How absolutely impossible it is to make our crooked life-story straight before God by our own unaided strength.

In a very impressive manner this was made clear to the disciples by the Lord in His parable of the wicked servant. He spoke of a king one of whose slaves owed him ten thousand talents, and he forgave him the whole debt (Matt. 18: 23–24). Ten thousand talents would have a value of about three million pounds sterling in gold. The buying power would be, however, much greater, needing to be multiplied many times.

We must compare these values with the monetary and wage values of those times in order to understand the great force of this parable. One talent consisted of 6,000 *denarii*. This means that 10,000 talents were equal to 60 million *denarii*. Two chapters further on, in the parable of the workers in the vineyard we, learn that the daily wage for a worker in the harvest amounted to one *denarius, i.e.,* not quite a shilling (Matt. 20: 2–10, 13). This means that the servant concerned, had he had to earn his money in the harvest-field as a labourer, would have had to work 60 million days solely to work off the capital amount which he owed his king and lord. Or shall we put it even more plainly: He would have had to work 164,000 *years* without holidays, without any Sundays or other furlough. And even then he would have worked off only the capital amount without having paid the interest, simple or compound interest, which of course would have to be reckoned up and added. Even if the rate of interest had been very small it would have cost much more than the few *denarii* which the debtor would have been able to earn. So that the more he worked to *de*crease his debt, the more his debt would have been *in*creased from day to day. Thus it becomes clear why the Lord used this tremendous, almost alarming comparison.[1] He purposely names such a huge figure. He wants to make it clear to us that our guilt before God is *so* immensely great! It is impossible to pay it off by our own efforts. Self-redemption is absolutely insufficient and out of the question. On the other hand, God's mercy is so wonderful that it exceeds all earthly relationships and comparisons. Jesus paid the ransom price for our huge guilt of sins of omission and commission. He did it on Golgotha. What a redemption! What a Saviour!

But then we must remember what duties this brings with it, even to serve Him in love and to show the same attitude of mind which corresponds to God's nature and God's forgiving goodness.

Therefore, if you have not yet taken Him as your personal Saviour, do not hesitate any longer. Do it now. He does not want to rob you of anything. He only wishes to give you something. He does not wish to impoverish you but to enrich you. Faith does not make poor, but rich.

> There is life in a look at the Crucified One,
> There is life at this moment for thee!

Let us look unto Jesus!

---

[1] *Cf.* similar figures of speech used by the Lord when He speaks of the "beam" in the eye of the hypocrite (Matt. 7: 3), of the "eye of the needle," through which a camel should pass (Matt. 19: 24), or of the "plucking out" of the right eye and of the "cutting off" of the right hand, which would be better than to sin (Matt. 5: 29, 30).

CHAPTER III

THE ANCIENT GREEK RACECOURSE AND THE SPIRITUAL WARFARE
(as compared in the New Testament)

"Know ye not that they which run in a race run all, but one receiveth the prize? Even so run, that ye may attain!" (I Cor. 9: 24.)

"Not that I have already obtained: but *I press on*. . . . Forgetting the things which are behind, and stretching forward to the things which are before, *I press on* toward the goal!" (Phil 3: 12–14.)

P EOPLES are organisms with soul and body. They are more than a mere sum total of individuals. They live a common corporate life through generations. Therefore each, according to its natural character, had definite ideals and goals.

I. GREEK AND ROMAN SPORT LIFE IN GENERAL

Freedom, beauty, and wisdom were the three chief ideals of the Greeks. They were therefore the goal of all Greek education. According to the ideal Greek conception a properly sound spirit can dwell only in a sound body. The Greek could scarcely think of a beautiful spirit in an ugly body. "*Mens sana in corpore sano.*" (Lat.) Therefore to true education belonged not only the exercise of mental characteristics, such as courage, activity, prudence, knowledge, art, but likewise the strengthening of the body through regular physical exercise. This should develop strength, dexterity, physical beauty, and, in conjunction with the higher spiritual training, conduce to the highest human excellence.

1. *The Greek ideal for soul and body.* For the Greek, beauty and virtue were inseparable. They saw the ideal man in the conjunction of a noble soul with a beautiful body. In his language the word for "beautiful" (Gk. *kalos*) meant also "good." Everything beautiful must be also good. Indeed, for this duality he coined a special double word, which comes in no other human language, *kalokagathia*. This is a union of the

three words: *kalos* beautiful, *kai* and *agathos* good; meaning thus equally "the beauty of goodness," or reversed, "the goodness of beauty." This word expressed his highest goal of ideal manhood, and was therefore of great significance in the Greek language. It indicated the harmonious and full cultivation of man in body and spirit.

The whole Greek life of sport served this goal. Both beauty of mind and strength and dexterity of body should be developed and directed to this harmonious ideal. Therefore the Greeks esteemed the cultivation of the body as not less important than that of the soul, and as early as the time of the poet Homer (about 900 B.C.) not to be experienced in gymnastics was considered a disgrace. Later the cultivation of gymnastics was made a State institution and was regulated by strict laws. These exercises, with graded degrees of difficulty, were carried on from the seventh year of life, until manhood was reached. They took place, if possible, every day. They were connected with bathing and swimming in cold river-water, and with a simple natural manner of life. This was all well-qualified to produce that beauty of body at which we still wonder in the old Grecian statues. In Sparta, where the gymnastic exercises were ordered more with a view to hardening for military service, the girls also were developed by running, spear throwing, and wrestling, so as to become the healthy mothers of a race of soldiers.

At all times gymnastics flourished among the Greeks, and were nurtured and celebrated. Only later did a manifold degeneration set in, so that by the practical Romans the whole system was not regarded with favour.

Into that Greek-Roman Mediterranean world the apostles carried the gospel of Jesus Christ. "Jesus is Saviour" was their message. It is He who frees from the guilt and the power of sin. Faith in Him creates new life, solves all problems, gives joy and strength, grants a victorious life, a living hope, and an eternal glorious goal. Therefore Christ is the revelation of the saving power of God. Where He reveals himself the powers of darkness are conquered. The gospel is the "power of God" (Rom. 1: 16).

But this power is not mechanical. Only by continuous union with Christ, as Himself the fount of power, will it be revealed in this world in the life of the redeemed. But the efficient working of the Holy Spirit, Who is the imparter of this power, is bound up with the personal devotion and earnest striving of the believer.   It will call forth in us a holy zeal, a stretching forth of oneself after holiness and victory.

"Right" and "power" were the two special and chief ideals of the Roman people, who at that time ruled the Mediterranean world.   "Right" and "power" were likewise two prominent verities and possessions of Christian truth.   Especially in Paul's teaching were they central.   For the gospel is the fulfilment of all human longing.   What Greeks and Romans strove after, what in general slumbered in the soul of each man as the goal of his innermost desire, became in Christ a living effective spiritual reality.   But at the same time this gift of God surpasses all conception of men in general, even as heaven is higher than earth, as God's mercy is greater than our need, as His strength is more glorious than all we could wish or hope for, even our greatest and highest.

To proclaim this salvation of God to men, and to help them to understand these mighty truths out of eternity, the apostles and evangelists of the Lord constantly used pictures and comparisons drawn from the civil, social, and cultural life of their time. And because discipleship to Christ is at the same time a holy war they often took their comparisons from the life of a soldier or an athlete.   Each hearer of their message, each reader of their letters should be made to perceive clearly that faith in Christ implied entrance into a conflict.   Now it is for us, in the power of God, to press towards the heavenly goal.   Now must we concentrate every power which God grants upon a divine aim.   Now must we fight and wrestle, not indeed in our own strength, but by the faith that makes use of the power of grace.   Only so can complete victory be secured.

Therefore it is important to be acquainted with the chief features of athletic practice of that period, so as to understand the numerous references to it in the New Testament.

2.   *The Greek "Gymnasium." The "Palaestra." The "Academy"* *at Athens.*   At first Greek gymnastics consisted of only a few exercises of the simplest type.   Thanks to the sunny climate of Greece these were practised in the open air and naked, on which latter account they were styled "gymnastics" (Gk. *gumnos*, naked). Consequently the place of exercise was called a "gymnasium." The gymnasia were airy and shady places with arrangements for games, races, and wrestling.   In the middle there was an open space (Gk. *ephebeion*) surrounded by colonnades (Gk. *peristylon*).

At great cost the gymnasia were adorned with statues and other works of art.

Later, special covered wrestling places were erected. These were termed Palaestra, which word is derived from the Greek word *palē*, wrestling contest. This word (from *pallo*, to sway, swing, whirl) pictures the wrestlers locked in each other's arms and swaying to and fro, each straining to throw the other. It is employed by Paul in his description of the armour of the Christian: "Our wrestling (*pale*) is not against flesh and blood, but against the principalities, against the powers, against the world-rulers of this darkness" (Eph. 6: 12).

In Athens the *palaestrae* were nearer to the city than were the *gymnasia*.

Racecourses were introduced (Gk. *stadion*). A stadium was about 200 yards in length. In the golden age of Greece, before the Peloponnesian war (431–404 B.C.), there arose many large and well-appointed gymnasia and palaestrae which, in addition to the ordinary arrangements, had special rooms for oiling and dusting the bodies of the wrestlers, baths, sweating chambers, and cloak-rooms. Near Athens there were three, and later five, such gymnasia, which were surrounded with gardens and adorned with images of gods.

According to their ideal of *kalokagathia*, the beauty of goodness, however, exercise of the body and training of the spirit were inseparably connected. This is the reason why just in these gymnasia there developed a powerful intellectual life. They were furnished with special rooms (Gk. *exedra*) for learned intercourse, in which philosophers, rhetoricians, and other scholars gathered for discussion, and which were provided with stone benches round the wall. The activity of Socrates, as described by Plato and Xenophon, gives a lively view of the mental life which developed in these schools, in addition to gymnastics.

One of the most celebrated of these schools was a gymnasium dedicated to the legendary hero Akademos and therefore called "Academy." This Akademos is mentioned in a by no means insignificant passage of the legend of king Theseus of Athens and the Dioscuri (the twin sons of Jupiter, Castor and Pollux. See Acts 28: 11). The king had stolen Helen, the sister of the Twins, but Akademos had revealed to the two brothers the spot where she was kept, so that they could recover her. Later, on account of this legend, the Lacedaemonians, who especially revered the Dioscuri, whenever they invaded Attica, always

c

spared this school dedicated to Akademos. It stood in the midst of pleasant gardens planted with plane and olive trees. In it was an altar sacred to the Muses, the goddesses of song. There was also a shrine of the goddess Athene. In the rooms of this Academy the philosopher Plato had taught. Aristotle taught in another school near Athens, called the Lykeion. Because Plato, and his pupils after him, taught in the Academy, his philosophical system was called the School of the Academicians. Even by enemies the Academy was spared. Sulla, the great opponent of Pompey, was the first to use the trees to make his war machines.

Because the schools of sport, the gymnasia, were devoted to the mental training of youth, and not to the bodily training alone, the Humanists of centuries fifteen and sixteen applied the term Gymnasium to their schools, since these were devoted in the first place to the cultivation of the ancient languages. This became the general title of high schools, especially in Germany. From the name of the Athenian palaestra Lykeion where Aristotle taught, the word "lyceum" is derived. Thus behind this usage stands the Greek conjunction of bodily and mental training in the sense of the chief ideal of the ancient Greeks, the *kalokagathia*.

The significance of the gymnasia and palaestra was heightened by the national games, for they were a field in which the dexterity gained in the palaestra could be displayed before all Greece and be duly honoured.

3. *The Olympian and Isthmian Games.* Because gymnastic exercises by their very nature were often competitive, every opportunity was used for arranging contests, especially at military triumphs, harvest festivals, and the dedication of temples. These contests were at first quite simple in style, but in the course of time they developed in sundry places into great, popular, national festivals. These were visited not only by the Greeks of the motherland, but also by the Hellenes of the Islands, and the Greeks dwelling on the western coast of Asia Minor, in south Italy, and in Egypt. The earliest centre of these festivals was Olympia.

Olympia was situated in the region of Elis, only a few hours from the coast of the Aegean Sea, against the island Zakynthos (Zante). Since the eighth century B.C. there had been arranged here every four years, at the summer solstice, five days of contests in honour of Zeus (Jupiter). The four years interval between the Olympian games formed an Olympiad.

Throughout Greece the victors were honoured and celebrated by songs and statues. Thus the Olympian games were at once the flower and the chief impetus of Greek gymnastics. Greeks by thousands streamed together to the Olympian games from all Greek territories and distant colonies, indeed, from the farthest removed regions to which Grecian culture had penetrated. Special dignity was conferred on the festival by embassies from the individual States, in which they sent their most distinguished men. Thus Olympia became the most definite expression of the national unity of the various Greek tribes, and was consequently the centre not only of the Peloponnesus but of the whole of Hellas.

Around these contests there developed also great fairs, with exchange of various wares. At the same time these festivals were used for all kinds of advertising. Especially after the 80th Olympiad (456 B.C.) poets, orators and artists sought to make their productions known before so select an audience. Even the renowned Greek historian Herodotus is reported to have read here in public a portion of his history of the Persian wars.

In addition to the Olympian games there were three other great national contests, but these never gained the same importance as the Olympian.

The *Isthmian* games were a festival of Ionians, and stood at first under the oversight of Athens and then of Corinth. The word "isthmus" signifies a narrow neck of land. It denoted here the narrow strip near Corinth which joins the mainland of Greece and the peninsula of Peloponnesus. In I Cor. 9: 20–27, Paul refers to these Isthmian games. The apostle was ever concerned to present his message to men in such form as they could most easily understand, and therefore his many symbolical references to the features of the current civilization. He would become all things to all men so as to win some to Christ (I Cor. 9: 19–23). So he became to the Jews as a Jew, to the Greeks as a Greek; to the Athenians as an Athenian, when, for instance, in his speech on Areopagus he referred to their altar (Acts 17: 23). And thus would he be to the Corinthians also a Corinthian, making detail use, in his letter to the Christians of that city, of the boxing and racing of the Isthmian games in their neighbourhood: "Know ye not that they who run in a race run all, but one receiveth the prize? Even so run, that ye may attain. And every man that striveth in the games is temperate in all things. Now they do it to receive a corruptible crown [*lit.* wreath]; but we an incorruptible. I therefore so run, as not uncertainly; so fight I, as not beating the air: But I buffet my body and bring it into bondage [*lit.* enslave it]: lest by any means, after that I have preached to others, I myself should be rejected" (I Cor. 9: 24–27).

The Isthmian games were held in honour of Poseidon the god of the sea. Their site was a spruce grove dedicated to him.

The *Pythian* games were held near Delphi, in the region of Phocis, near the foot of Mount Parnassus. Delphi was the chief oracle of the sun god Apollo. They were held in his honour. It was a "Pythonic" spirit, a medium of the heathen god, that Paul, by special appeal to the name of the Lord Jesus Christ, cast out of the fortune-teller at Philippi (Acts 16: 16–18).

The Pythian games commenced in the year 586 B.C. At first they were musical competitions, and were songs accompanied by playing the cithara, lute, and lyre (a form of the guitar), and later the flute. Afterward gymnastic contests were added, such as chariot and horse races. As the laurel was sacred to the sun god Apollo, the victor's garland at Delphi was twisted out of laurel, the branches of which had been carried in advance in solemn procession out of the hallowed laurel grove. Besides that the victor received a branch of palm, as was often the case at the Olmpian games.

The fourth chief Grecian games were held at *Nemea* in the district of Argolis. They were celebrated in honour of Zeus, but did not attain any widespread importance.

In Paul's time athletic games were held in most Roman provinces. Almost every city had its regularly recurring contests, the organization of which belonged to the most important duties of the local authorities. Ephesus, which for Paul, and later for John, was one of the most important centres of evangelistic work, was the capital of the Roman province of Asia, in west Asia Minor. The President of the highest Council of the Province was both high priest and also umpire of the games. He was one of the "Asiarchs."[1] As senior officials these were presidents of the public festivals, which had a religious character.

Such sporting festivals were held in almost all the cities to which the seven letters in the book of *Revelation* were addressed,

[1] Some of these Asiarchs had friendly relations with Paul (Acts 19: 31).

for example, Ephesus, Smyrna, Sardis, Philadelphia, Laodicea
(Rev. 2 and 3).   Thus these customs and practices were known in
the whole world surrounding the early Christians, so that it is
easily understood why the writers of the New Testament so often
refer to them as pictures and comparisons to make their message
clear and comprehensible to their Christian readers.

4. *Olympia as central Greek National Shrine.*   In ancient times
Olympia was a sacred place, with beautiful plantations, numerous
buildings, and adorned with thousands of statues.   The flourishing province of Olympia and Elis was granted permanent freedom from war.   No armed force dared to cross its boundary.
While the Olympian games were being celebrated, there had to
be cessation of hostilities all over Greece.   It was thus ordained
as early as the time of the Spartan lawgiver Lycurgus, about
850 B.C.   It was proclaimed by the heralds, and during the whole
period of the festival applied to all contending parties in Greece.

The festival fell in the time of the new moon after the summer
solstice, about the beginning of July.   When to the simple races
other contests were added, the duration of the games was gradu-
ally extended from one day to five.

In the year 776 B.C. a certain Koroibos won the race.   Thence-
forward the name of the victor was registered.   This year was
also the beginning of the reckoning of the Olympiads.   An
Olympiad was the four-year interval from festival to festival.
But this reckoning did not apply to the common civil life.

The most flourishing period of the Olympian games was in the
sixth and fifth centuries B.C., until the Peloponnesian war (431–
404).   But in spite of all the conflicts between the Grecian tribes
they continued, and even under the Roman rule.   Indeed,
Roman Emperors, as Nero, sought to gain the honour of the
Olympian Victor's wreath.

Right at the entrance to the central sacred circle stood the
holy wild olive tree (Gk. *elaia kallistephanos*) from which were
taken the twigs for the victor's wreath.   Close by was the vast
temple of the Olympian Zeus.   Floors, columns, and statues
were found in place and are now in the Museum of Olympia.
In the temple was the greatest and finest example of Hellenistic
sculpture, the statue of Olympian Zeus.   According to the
description of Herodotus it was the handiwork of Phidias, of
gold and ivory.

The Olympian games continued in changed form until the

fourth century after Christ, when they were forbidden by the emperor Theodosius, as a relic of heathendom. This was in A.D. 394, that is, after the 293rd Olympiad.

Temple and pillared halls were destroyed by earthquakes. The river Altheios overflowed and choked the racecourse and arenas. Especially after the downfall of the Roman empire all that remained of the splendid buildings was destroyed by devastation and plunder, so that scarcely a trace was left. Thus natural catastrophes and the neglect of centuries turned into an unwholesome wild plain, covered with low bushes, this most splendid place, formerly covered with lovely groves, numerous buildings, and thousands of statues, a place of daily religious sacrifice. Only in the nineteenth century did it again, by careful toil, become fruitful, and now fields of maize and barley, vineyards and olive trees cover the once sacred district of Elis.

An Englishman, Chandler (1776), first directed attention to Olympia. The actual excavations were carried out by German scholars, namely, Professor Curtius, tutor of the Emperor Frederick III, and his fellow-worker, Professor Adler (1875–1881). The sculptures, bronzes and architectural specimens found are preserved in the great Museum at Olympia, built by order of the King of Greece after the plans of Adler. The writer of this book possesses an original watercolour painting by Adler of Olympia and the Museum. Through the excavations of Curtius and Adler an exact survey of the sacred buildings and monuments has become possible.

5. *Amphitheatres and circuses of the Romans: Circus Maximus and Colosseum at Rome.* The games and contests of the Romans bore another stamp. With them the amphitheatre and the circus were the characteristic places.

The Roman amphitheatre was an oval or circular building, without roof, with surrounding rows of seats forming ascending steps. The interior space was separated by a wall from the area of seats. It was strewn with sand and was the scene of the contests. It was therefore called the arena (Lat., *arena,* sand). It was surrounded by cages for the beasts and rooms for the combatants. The lowest row of seats was for the umpires of the games. The place of honour was the *Podium.* Here sat the Institutor of the games, and likewise the vestals, the priestesses of the State and of the goddess Vesta. Next above were the seats of the senators, the knights, and the people. For protection from the sun and rain large awnings (Lat. *velaria*) could be drawn over the heads of the onlookers. The author has seen in the amphitheatre at Pompeii the iron rings which held the hooks for these great awnings.

Vast crowds gathered to these games in the amphitheatre. Even the night before the games the people streamed there to secure seats: for though the space was so vast it was nevertheless difficult to find room. The Flavium Amphitheatrum, built by the Emperors Vespasian and Titus, the so-called Colosseum, in Rome, had over 50,000 seats. That of Scaurus held 80,000 persons. From literature or from ruins a total of some 270 Roman amphitheatres are known. They were found all over the Roman Empire. Near Brugg, in north Switzerland, the writer visited a small amphitheatre of the Roman period for about 6,000 persons. At Pompeii near Naples, where there was an amphitheatre for 5,000 people, we sat on an ancient spectator's bench.

Such an amphitheatre must have been a splendid sight. Every seat would be occupied. Beneath, the nobility, senators, senior officers, ladies in richest apparel sparkling with gold and jewels. The Vestal priestesses of the State in priestly attire. Far above sat the common people, the peasantry, the soldiers—even slaves had free access. High over the arena an awning was spread; coloured carpets decorated the balustrades; flags flew on their staffs; garlands of roses climbed from pillar to pillar. Between were shining statues of the gods, before which stood bowls of incense. Often figs, dates, nuts, and cakes were thrown among the people, as well as roasted fowls and pheasants. Lotteries were distributed, by which could be won garments, furniture, gold, silver, even houses and estates. In one day a lucky man could become rich. Everything breathed of pleasure and happiness. They laughed and joked, spun love-stories, and made bets for or against each contestant: yet what a horrid spectacle it was that the crowd awaited!

The other place of the Roman games was the *circus*. The name comes from the Latin word *circus* = circle; but its form was not a circle, but a wide far-stretching racecourse. There was racing, boxing, and wrestling at the great Circensian Games (Lat. *Ludi Circenses*), which were known everywhere in the Mediterranean world. It is these contests which Paul not seldom uses as pictures of the conflicts of the spiritual life.

The largest circus was the Circus Maximus in Rome. According to tradition it was built by king Tarquin Priscus about 500 B.C. in the valley between the Palatine and the Aventine hills. Caesar completed the arena, which was some 700 yards in length and 140 in breadth. It was enclosed by three tiers of arcades. Within there were the rows of seats for the spectators. Here also the lower rows were for the senators and the higher classes. The royal box was beneath. In the time of Caesar the number of seats is reported to have run to 150,000. In the time of Titus, the conqueror of Jerusalem, they were given as 250,000. In century four this had risen to 385,000. Even if there may have been certain exaggerations in the Greek and Roman reports, it is manifest that the numbers must have been tremendously great. The circus was unroofed, but as in the amphitheatre, spectators could be protected from the sun by outspread awnings.

Among the Romans, besides foot-racing, wrestling, and boxing, horse and chariot races played an important part, and to a large extent also fights of wild beasts. They were more prominent than foot-racing. Indescribably ferocious and lustful spectacles took place in both the circus and the amphitheatre of the Roman world in the time of the Emperors.

In the great Hellenistic cities, the manner of life of the masses, who did little or no work, became more and more degenerate. *Panem et circenses*—Bread and games!—these they demanded from their rulers. By day they stood about idle: in the evening they went to the amphitheatre, this disgusting invention of Roman brutality. In addition to this there came a senseless exaggeration of sport. The mad emperor Caligula could without risk think of nominating his favourite horse Incicatus to be Consul(!), and thus the chief officer of State. The emperor Nero himself appeared as charioteer, singer, musician, and poet, and toured the provinces with a senseless display of splendour as an actor and stage performer.

In the amphitheatre, before thousands upon thousands of spectators, the gladiators (Lat. *gladius*, sword) fought for life or death. If one spared himself he was driven on with red-hot rods. Great was the enthusiasm when one picturesquely fell in the battle, while thousands applauded. Caesar caused not only that man should fight with man but that bands should encounter bands; 300 horsemen against 300 horsemen, 500 footmen against 500 footmen, 20 elephants against 20 elephants. After the completion of the amphitheatres, especially after the time of Caesar, the wild beast conflicts were more often performed there, rather than in the circuses.

Water was let into special basins, and the spectators were treated to regular sea-fights. Whole flotillas contended. The emperor Claudius (mentioned in Acts 11: 28; 18: 2) gave on the Fucin lake a spectacular sea-fight between galleys with three banks of rowers and those with four, seating altogether 19,000 men. Domitian, the contemporary of the apostle John, caused a new and still greater lake to be dug, on which fought fleets in full war array. All this was not mimic war, but real fighting in which thousands fell or were drowned.

If these displays might in some sense have given a certain impression of magnificence, the execution of criminals, which also took place among the shows in the amphitheatre, could offer only the exhibition of the horrible and vulgar. Bound to stakes, the condemned were completely defenceless against starving wild beasts. Sometimes they were allowed weapons, but only to the prolonging of their torment. Robbers, hanging on crosses, were torn limb from limb by bears. Often these executions were given a theatrical, mythological and dramatic form, wherein the condemned played the part of some dying hero of heathen legend or stories of the gods. One saw Mucius Scaevola hold his hand over a bowl of burning coal or Hercules mount the pyre and burn.

Later, very possibly in the time of Nero, and so of Paul, this dramatic, mythological form of execution was applied also to Christians. The crowd delighted when the martyrs were made to play the part of Hercules, who was burnt, or of Ixion, who was broken on the wheel, or of Marsyas, whose skin was stripped from his living body. Women must appear as Dirce, who according to tradition was tied by the hair to a bull and dragged to death. Such suffering is reported of the renowned martyr Perpetua near Carthage (A.D. 202). Others had to represent the Danaids who must ceaselessly pour water into leaky vessels, driven on by the lash until they collapsed and died.

Usually the bloody spectacle began with a parade of gladiators in full armour. Before the Emperor and his suite they laid down their weapons and cried, "*Ave, Caesar; morituri te salutant!*" "Hail, O Caesar; those about to die greet thee!"

First came a mimic battle. Then the trumpets gave the signal, and the fight with sharp weapons began. Gladiators stepped forward, singly or in bands, with sword, dagger, or net. Horsemen with long lances charged one another.   Others fought from chariots.

If one fell alive into the hand of his opponent, the spectators decided for life or death.   If they waved their kerchiefs or held their thumbs upward, then life was granted.   But if they turned their thumbs downward that was the order for the death-stroke. Even light-minded and frivolous women and girls gave the sign that sent a man to death.

In all parts of the world wild beasts were hunted to provide for the amphitheatre.   From Egypt they brought the hippopotamus, from Germania the wild boar, from Africa the lion, from India the elephant.   Hundreds of beasts reached the arena.   Six hundred bears and 500 lions are mentioned at one festival.   At the games with which the emperor Trajan (shortly after the time of the apostle John) celebrated his victory over the Dacians in A.D. 106, there fought in all 11,000 wild beasts.   In the 120 days of the games at the dedication of the Colosseum at Rome 12,000 beasts and 10,000 gladiators lost their lives.

When the first blood flowed there rose the roar of the crowd and their cries of approval.   There was downright thirst for blood.   Even before the defeated had time to appeal for mercy the cry for blood resounded and the stroke followed that ended life.   Slaves, in the garb of the god of the underworld, dragged the still convulsing bodies into the room of the dead.   This was done by hooks thrust into the breast.   The victors received palm branches, gifts of money, and costly foods.   They were "satiated," made "rich," and treated as the "kings" of the day (*cf.* I Cor. 4: 8).

In the intervals the bloodsoaked sand was shovelled from the arena.   Negroes scattered fresh sand, scented water was sprinkled. Then the bloodshedding began afresh.

To keep up the nervous excitement by ever keener stimulus, the items of the programme became ever sharper and bloodier.   The "last" conflicts were the most terrible and exciting.

All this must one keep in mind to understand certain expressions of the picture language as it is employed in the letters of Paul, especially in his first epistle to the Corinthians when he warns them against self-security and self-exaltation.

6.   *The Roman Amphitheatre and Paul's figurative language.*   "For I think that God hath set forth us the apostles *last* of all, as men doomed to death: for we are made a *spectacle* unto the world and

to angels and men.   We are fools for Christ's sake, but ye are
wise in Christ; we are weak, but ye are strong: ye have glory but
we have dishonour. . . . Already ye are *filled* (satiated), already
ye are become *rich*, ye have *reigned* without us" (I Cor. 4: 9,
10, 8).

Observe the words "spectacle" (Gk. *theatron*), "filled"
(satiated), "rich," "reigning as kings" (feeling as if one were a
king), set forth as the "last."   In this particular bringing together of the terms may there not lie a special view-point of the
apostle?   Indeed, in these remarks of Paul, in which, by use of
holy irony, he contends against the pride of the Corinthians, it
appears that he has in mind the proceedings in the games in the
arena.   He compares the Corinthians and himself with those who
step out into the circus or amphitheatre.   At the start came the
lighter and less dangerous combats.   The last items on the programme became the fiercest contests when it was a matter of life
and death.   Also the execution of criminals condemned to die
took place, as we saw, in the arena in broad theatrical publicity.

Paul compares the Corinthian Christians to those who entered
the arena at the beginning, who had the easier battles, and thus,
of course, had usually finished their contests first.   *They* apparently had already won their victory, while he had still to fight.
So in holy irony he says: *You* have already received your gifts,
even as the victorious combatants in the arena were richly rewarded by coins flung down by the lookers on: "you are rich."
You have already had your feast, even as the fighters in the arena
who conquered had a great meal: "you are filled" (satiated).
You have been already honoured and feel yourselves to be kings:
"ye have reigned as kings."

But all this did not alter the fact that these so haughty, self-
conceited Corinthians had faced only the *easier* battles.   Therefore their wrestlings and apparent victories were only like the
first, the easier part of the programme of the spectacle (*theatron*)
in the arena.   But Paul and his fellow-workers had to maintain
the harder battle.   Theirs was like the *last* items of the programme.   They were *epithanatioi*, that is, gladiators, whose
contest ended in life or death, or those who were adjudged to
die, and so to experience the worst.   Their battle was more
serious than that of those who suppose all is so simple, so matter
of course, so secure.   His devotion was more definite; he did
not shirk the hardest fight.   Therefore he goes on to say: "Even
unto this present hour we both hunger, and thirst, and are naked,

and are buffeted, and have no certain dwelling-place; and we toil, working with our own hands: being reviled, we bless; being persecuted, we endure; being defamed, we entreat; we are made as the filth of the world, the offscouring of all things, even until now. I write not these things to shame you, but to admonish you as my beloved children" (I Cor. 4: 11–14).

There is another reference to the spectacles in the arena of circus and amphitheatre in this word of the apostle in the same letter: "If after the manner of men I fought with beasts at Ephesus, what doth it profit me? If the dead are not raised, let us eat and drink, for tomorrow we die" (I Cor. 15: 32).

Doubtless Paul had not literally had to fight with wild beasts in the amphitheatre at Ephesus. There are two reasons for this, Paul was a Roman citizen, and according to Roman law no one who possessed this citizenship could be condemned to fight with beasts. Moreover Paul would not have failed to mention this when enumerating his sufferings in the second letter to Corinth (11: 23–28), for just this would have been the strongest testimony of all hardships which in this respect had befallen the apostle.

So that the expression can only be figurative. In Ephesus Paul had encountered rough and dangerous men, who had acted towards him like wild beasts. In his letter to the Romans, Ignatius of Antioch similarly described the heathen crew of the ship on which he was taken from Syria to Rome there to be tried and then executed in the Colosseum (about A.D. 112). He wrote: "From Syria to Rome by land and sea I fought with wild beasts, day and night, chained to ten leopards. These were the soldiers who with every kindness shown to them became only the more malicious."

Furthermore, by his remark, "I have fought with wild beasts in Ephesus," Paul cannot have meant the uproar of the silversmith Demetrius and the stupid, unbridled raging of the thoughtless, excited mob in the theatre (Acts 19: 23–34). For Paul had indeed written the first letter to Corinth in Ephesus (I Cor. 16: 8); but this was a few weeks *before* Pentecost in a situation in which quite apparently no special outward disturbances affected his work. But according to the account in Acts (20: 1), immediately after that tumult he left Ephesus, so that there was no time to compose so long and weighty a letter as the first epistle to Corinth.

Therefore that letter must have been written earlier, and his reference to fighting with wild beasts must refer to previous

experiences. The passage can only be understood either that
Paul had in mind some special single attack in Ephesus of which
we do not know, or that he desired to indicate in general that
everywhere raging enemies had surrounded him, so that he himself had always afresh risked his life for Christ's sake. But all
this he had been enabled to do and suffer only in view of the
resurrection and perfecting, the triumph of the work of Christ
and the glory of the world to come. Therefore only faith in
the resurrection gave him the strength to devote himself so fully
and wholly to his Lord and Redeemer.

Without the amphitheatre that world of the apostle is simply
not to be imagined. Also as regards the names of the twenty-five
brethren and sisters of the church in Rome found in the saluta-
tions of the apostle at the close of his epistle to the Romans, we
shall certainly not be mistaken if we say that not a few of those
greeted ended their earthly life in the arena. The persecution
of the Christians by Nero (A.D. 64) broke out only a very few
years after the letter to the Romans was written. Now it is
always the faithful who are the first to be persecuted, so that it
may be taken for granted that not a few became martyrs for
Christ whom Paul described here as "fellow-workers in Christ
Jesus . . . beloved in the Lord . . . fellow-prisoners . . . approved
in Christ . . . who laboured much in the Lord" (Rom. 16: 3, 5, 7,
8, 9, 10, 12). Over Romans 16 flames the awful glare of the
burning of Rome and the terrifying brightness of human torches
in the nightly illumination of the Emperor's palace gardens and
the Circus of Nero.

But let us never forget that the witnesses of the martyr church
of the first centuries would not have been vigorous enough to
offer up their lives in full devotion to Christ even unto death
unless they had previously lived a life of consecration and testimony. They would never have been able to die and conquer
in the arena of the amphitheatres had they not proved steadfast
and true in the arena of faith.

Only he who proves faithful in the practical tests of daily
life can stand fast in the great tests and trials of special situations.
Only he who conquers in the ordinary will be able to conquer
in the extraordinary. Only he who is faithful in the small
things can be faithful in the great (Luke 16: 10). But such
an one will then also have the blessed experience "as thy days, so
thy strength" (Deut. 33: 25). To the faithful the Lord will grant
special accessions of His strength in special circumstances. But

faithfulness and devotion are prerequisites for all Divine gifts and blessings.

Therefore despise not the commonplace. Do not under-estimate the need of being victorious in the small burdens and tests. Mere admiration and enthusiasm for those heroic martyrs in the time of the ancient Roman emperors does not help us today. We should not only look on and admire but be practical followers of their faithfulness and devotion to Christ. Faith in final vic-tory involves responsibility to live victoriously today. The heroism of Christ's witnesses in the arena of circus and amphi-theatre should be to us an unforgettable spur to self-denial, endurance, and steadfast striving towards the goal, in the arena of faith. This is the reason why in our present exposition we have given so detailed a description of the circus and amphi-theatre. We obtain insight into the surroundings of the early Christians. We understand certain New Testament allusions and references to those conditions. But we are thereby also impres-sively called to unreserved devotion of our own life to Christ. Thus shall we be runners in the race, followers of Christ's wit-nesses of former times, and shall together with them become partakers of the coming final glorious victory. "Therefore seeing we are compassed about with so great a cloud of wit-nesses . . . let us run with patience the race that is set before us" (Heb. 12: 1). Let us consecrate our life to Christ! Let us press on in the arena of faith (Heb. 6: 1).

7. *The Cross in the Colosseum.* Years ago we were in the Colosseum. It is the site where formerly the Golden House (Lat. *Domus Aurea*) of Nero stood, a vast palace with many villas and gardens, fountains and lakes, and halls adorned with gold, marble, and ivory. It was the scene of Nero's persecution of Christians, where shortly after Paul's time they were killed in the most horrible ways. Fifteen years after Nero the emperors Vespasian and Titus, of the Flavian house, built the vast Flavian amphitheatre, the greatest example of Roman construction. The name Colosseum was given only later in the Middle Ages because of the nearness of a colossal statue of Nero (Lat. *Colossus Neronis*). By night the mighty ruins rear against the sky like a spectre. The most important walls, rows of seats, boxes, and doors can still be plainly recognized. We entered the former Imperial box and gained an impressive view. We saw the box where sat the Vestal priestesses in white robes, the priestesses of

the State, who had the chief decision for life or death of the defeated gladiators. We saw the great chambers with the railed cages where some 2,000 wild beasts were kept, lions, bears, elephants, giraffes, tigers, and other beasts of prey from Africa and Asia. On the left was the great arch of the Door of the Living (Lat. *Porta Sanavivaria,* door of health and life), through which passed the gladiators and martyrs to reach the arena. "Hail to thee, O Caesar; those about to die greet thee." A thousand times this had rung out before the Emperor's box. Opposite to it was the Door of Libertina, the door of the goddess of corpses, through which the fallen warriors or the dead martyrs were dragged with hooks. What a bloodthirsty ecstasy of the masses! What streams of martyr blood had flowed on this very spot in the two centuries from the time of the apostles. How helpless and feeble the small band of Christians then seemed. How did they appear to be doomed to utter destruction without deliverance. How small one feels, especially in such a place, when remembering all these heroes, without whom we of today would not possess the treasure of the gospel.

But what did we see in the arena, in the very centre, directly in front of the ruins of the royal box? A CROSS! A plain high cross! About the year 1300 a cross was erected here in memory of the martyrs. In the course of time it was lost. In the year 1927 it was again erected by order of the Italian Government, with this most significant inscription on its base: "*Ave crux spes unica,*" that is "Hail to thee, O Cross, the only hope!"

A cross in the Colosseum! Exactly where formerly believers on account of their testimony to the Crucified suffered a bloody death, exactly there a cross stands erect today, bearing this so simple but mighty inscription! The seats of the heathen mockers, the walls of the Colosseum itself, lie in ruins. On the place where God's witnesses died, in the middle of the arena, stands, like a sign of triumph, a victorious and lofty cross.

Three times I have been in the Colosseum: three times have I stood long and thoughtfully before this cross and its inscription.

Immediately before we had been in the Forum Romanum, the splendid market-place of ancient Rome. We had seen temples of the gods, noble halls, triumphal arches—all in ruins! We had walked over the *Via Sacra,* the holy street of processions and triumphs—but around were only ruins. Indeed, so completely was this centre of world empire later forgotten that, overgrown with rushes and bushes, it was used by the peasants to rest their oxen, and late in the Middle Ages was called "Cow pasture" (Italian *Campo Vaccino*, *cf.* Lat. *vacca,* cow).

But the band of the persecuted remain victors. Their faith in Christ was stronger than all the hate of their enemies. The cross, on account of which they suffered, became the symbol of triumph.

The temples of the heathen, and the palaces of their rulers, have sunk in dust; but the temple of the church remains. How is this?

It is because Christ, the Crucified, is also the Risen One: because in this His temple, the temple of the church, the true God dwells: because this house, though outwardly plain, is the royal house of the Eternal!

Thus history testifies: thus will at last eternity testify: and thus we also join in the testimony of the Colosseum cross, crying:

Hail to the, O Cross, the only hope!

From this confidence of victory we can draw fresh incentive to hasten joyfully forward to the heavenly goal. Because Christ has triumphed we also can conquer. His cross is at once the sign of victory, of duty, and of promise for all who believe on Him. Therefore faith in Him is both hope and assurance, and looking unto Him we can run with steadfastness the race of faith.

II. The Religious Character of Pagan Sport and Athletics

The Roman conflicts in amphitheatre and circus, like the earlier Greek sports, were intimately connected with faith in the heathen gods. The gymnastic games of the Greeks, as well as the later brutal and degenerate contests of the Romans, were instituted in the name and to the honour of the pagan godheads.

1. *Gymnastics as part of heathen worship in Greek and Roman life.* The Olympian games were in honour of Zeus (Jupiter), the Isthmian games near Corinth in honour of the sea god Poseidon, and the Pythian games in honour of the sun god Apollo.

The crowns of the victors corresponded. From the olive, sacred to Zeus, was taken the olive spray which crowned the victor at Olympia. From the laurel, sacred to Apollo, came the crown at Delphi. The victor at the Isthmian games was adorned with a wreath of spruce, the tree sacred to Poseidon.

Religious processions were connected with the contests at

Olympia. Sacrifices were offered by the representatives of the State and by individual victors. The whole district of Elis around Olympia was sacred to Zeus. In grove and temple were only objects that belonged to the gods.

The central object in Olympia was the great altar to Zeus. It was erected on a big stone base. It was formed out of the burnt leg-bones of the beasts offered, mixed with water from the river Alpheios and dried. Here sacrifices to Zeus were offered daily. South-west from the altar rose the Olympiēum, the celebrated temple of Olympian Zeus, built about 450 B.C. In its inner court stood the colossal statue of Zeus enthroned, the work of Phidias, the greatest Greek sculptor.

By the Romans also the chief games were held in honour of particular gods, especially of Jupiter, Apollo, Juno, Minerva, Diana, Pluto, and Proserpine, as well as in honour of Flora, the goddess of Spring, and to the Syrian Magna Mater (Great Mother), whose symbol, a stone fallen from heaven (a meteor), was brought in 205 B.C. to Rome and very quickly obtained high honour.

Some days before taking part in the games and contests men prepared themselves by prayers, sacrifices, and adorning the altars.

2. *Religious processions before the beginning of the Roman athletic combats.* There was often a parade before the games. At the Circensian games in Rome, with the sound of tubes (Lat. *tuba*, trumpet) and flutes, it went from the Capitol, across the Forum, through the middle of the City to the Circus Maximus. The senior Magistrate led the procession, followed by the statues of the gods on magnificent chariots. Smaller statues of gods were carried on the shoulder. Then came the appointed fighters, horses, chariots, both two- and four-horse, the priests, victims for sacrifice, dancers, flute players and harpists. At the Circus Maximus a sacrifice was offered. Then the actual games began, especially racing, boxing, wrestling, and horse and chariot races. Everything was associated with heathen religious dedication. Even at the close of the Republic, when religion fell more and more into decay, its outward form was maintained at these games, which were celebrated with ever-increasing splendour and glory.

3. *Introduction of Hellenistic Games in Jerusalem.* Because the Greco-Roman world combined athletics with religion, the con-

querors sought, especially from the second century before Christ, to employ them to break the religious strength of Judaism by the forcible introduction of such games in Palestine. Especially since the time of Antiochus Epiphanes (175–164 B.C.) there had been a party among the Jews who wished to obliterate the sharp frontier between them and the heathen. The high priest Jason, in particular, worked in this direction, not without result. There were priests who forsook the altar, neglected the sacrifices, and hastened to the arena to watch the games (II Macc. 4: 9ff.). This aroused the greatest horror in the Jews who were true to Jehovah. There was much strife and controversy concerning these games in Jerusalem, but in spite of all this they advanced considerably, especially under the influence of king Herod. He favoured them, for they belonged to Hellenism. He caused splendid amphitheatres and hippodromes to be built in Caesarea and Jericho, as Josephus narrates. He ordered that every four years a great sport festival should take place with special magnificence in honour of the emperor Augustus. Through all this quite naturally the knowledge of these Greek and Roman games spread among the Jews.

4.   *The New Testament writers and their detailed knowledge of Greek and Roman sport life and games.*   In the New Testament it is especially the writings of Paul, John, and the writer of *Hebrews*, that contain essential allusions and comparisons to the Greek games.   On one occasion Paul employs even an expressly technical sporting term *hypopiazo*, "I hit under the eye with the fist," I smite my opponent (I Cor. 9: 27).

But the early Christians did not obtain their knowledge of heathen sporting customs by visiting these institutions, or by personal participation in the games, *after* their conversion to Christ. For Paul even *before* his conversion a visit to these festivals was completely excluded.   For every orthodox Jew, to which company Paul as an earnest Pharisee belonged, such participation was forbidden in advance.   And John belonged to the "remnant" of Israel that waited for the Messiah, for whom also these heathen games must have been an abomination.

The ground for this lay in the religious character of these institutions.   The contests were indeed one with heathen religion.   During the festival the combatants were regarded as darlings of the gods.   Even Philo of Alexandria, the celebrated contemporary of Christ and the apostles, who so much sought to combine Greek thought and faith in Jehovah, mentions that only once in his life did he attend the games.

Therefore the New Testament writers did not gain their knowledge of these customs directly but indirectly, not by personal observation but by general hearing about them, not through participation but through the widespread knowledge and daily talk of their contemporaries. Nevertheless it is evident that scarcely a single essential feature of the whole course of the games has escaped their notice and not been employed in the New Testament figurative speech, especially with Paul. Here again is seen how the writers of the New Testament endeavoured to present their message to their hearers and readers in the most understandable form.

III. The Chief Different Kinds of Games

1. *The Race* (Gk. *stadion*). Of the different games the New Testament mentions three: racing, boxing, and wrestling. The race is mentioned most frequently.

There were also three other chief games: throwing the discus (Gk. *diskobolia*); throwing the spear (Gk. *akontismos*); and jumping (Gk. *halma*). Often jumping, spear-throwing, quoit-throwing, racing, and wrestling were united and formed the so-called "five-fold contest" (Gk. *pentathlon*). He who conquered in this was especially honoured.

With the 25th Olympiad began chariot racing, with two or four horses. Then horse racing was introduced. There was also a race in armour (Gk. *hoplites dromos*). The stadium was 600 feet in length.

In each of the three pictures of athletic life as employed in the New Testament there is prominent a special view-point of the spiritual life and effort.

The race looks *forward* to the heavenly goal, to the "high calling of God in Christ Jesus," to the realm above (Phil. 3: 14).

Boxing points to our opposition to the enemy *in* us. Paul at least so employs it: "so fight (*lit.* box) I, as not beating the air: but I buffet *my body*, and bring it into bondage" (I Cor. 9: 26, 27).

Wrestling refers to our fight with the powers of darkness *around* and *beneath* us. Thus Paul says: "Our wrestling (Gk. *palē*) is against the principalities, against the powers, against the world-rulers of this darkness" (Eph. 6: 12).

Thus these three comparisons, in spite of their great similarity, nevertheless picture three different directions of our Christian warfare.

The most important truths illustrated by the race are:

X   All *can* reach the goal.   Therefore, according to the will and by the power of God, it is possible for *you* also.

All must run and *hasten* with all available strength.   Therefore *you* also.

All must *concentrate* on the goal.   No one must be drawn aside by things passing or external.

All must *persevere* to the winning-post.   No one must yield to fatigue on the way.   Therefore *you* must be purposeful and hold out also.

All must press forward *without pause*.   No one must permit himself to be detained.

All must be careful not to *stumble* in this obstacle-race.   For Christ can preserve us.

All must be *determined* to win the noblest and highest, and in no case be content with reaching only lesser aims.   Therefore *you* also.

Thus will be richly supplied to us the entrance into the eternal kingdom of our Lord Jesus Christ (II Pet. 1: 11).   Thus will be apportioned to us the victor's prize, the full glory in the day of our manifestation before the judgment seat of Christ, the great heavenly Umpire (II Tim. 4: 8; II Cor. 5: 10).

We conceive that the picture of the race is particularly adapted to represent chief essential truths of Christian sanctification and the fight of faith, and therefore in the New Testament it is more used than any other comparison from the life of sport: (I Cor. 9: 24; Phil. 3: 14; II Tim. 4: 7; Acts 20: 24; Heb. 12: 1, 2; perhaps also Gal. 5: 7).

The direction of a man's thoughts is always the decisive factor in his personality.   His whole outer life will be determined by the inward inclination of his mind.   Therefore that spiritual renewing of man which Christ will effect consists in the inner movements of the will, the cogitations of the heart, the thoughts and endeavours of the soul being directed towards things heavenly and divine, to eternity, to Christ Himself.

Whether the heart so directed really strives *wholly* towards the right goal is shown as a rule when something meets us which would draw us aside, when we are tempted to look away from the goal, either sideways or even backwards.   Therefore Paul referring to the racecourse, says that in the fight of faith he ran as one who forgot the things behind and stretched forth unto that which was ahead (Phil. 3: 13).

And as a threefold brilliantly illuminated motto it shines forth from Philippians 3, this incomparable self-testimony of the apostle in which he applies the picture of the race to his own spiritual life and service, as he does in no other portion of his epistles so extensively and emphatically:

> The calling and strength of the racer—
> given entirely *by* Christ! (vv. 4–7).
> The ideal and the inward object of the racer—
> living only *for* Christ! (8–14).
> The blessed hope of the racer—
> to be for ever in glory *with* Christ (20, 21; comp. 14).

"For our citizenship is in heaven; whence also we wait for a Saviour, the Lord Jesus Christ" (20). Therefore "I press on toward the goal unto the prize of the high calling of God in Christ Jesus" (14).

2. *Boxing* (Gk. *pux, pugme*). This was one of the hardest contests, in which the combatants struck each other heavily, especially in the face. As early as Homer (about 900 B.C.) the hands were bound with thongs, leaving the fingers free. Later the *Caestus* was introduced. This, especially among the Romans, was a leather thong set with metal knobs, of lead or iron. This often inflicted terrible, indeed dangerous wounds. On this account the head, particularly the temples, was partly protected by a woollen or leathern cap (Gk. *amphotis*). The contest was decided when one of the boxers by lifting the hand acknowledged himself defeated. Thereupon the other dared not further attack him. In 684 B.C. boxing was introduced in the Olympian games.

Not seldom boxing and wrestling were united. This was the so-called "all-in (general) battle" (Gk. *pankration*). In this contest the hands were without thongs, and therefore the wounds were less dangerous than in boxing alone. Later this contest became a specially admired show-piece of the athletes. In Olympia it was introduced rather late (644 B.C.). Neither of these forms of boxing was practised by the Spartans.

The decisive blow was the "fist blow under the eye," for which there was a special technical term (Gk. *hup-opiazo, i.e., hupo,* under, *ops,* the eye). In the terminology of stadium and amphitheatre it meant the same as the present term "knock-out." In his use of pictures from the sport life Paul goes so far that in his reference in his first epistle to the Corinthians to the contest, especially to those that took place near Corinth, the Isthmian games, he plainly applies the technical expression, "I buffet my body" (*hup-opiazo*): "I give it the fist blow under the eye: I beat my body and defeat it." This means that the Christian has to pay no heed to himself. If his own "I," its wishes and longings, its convenience and enjoyment, are a hindrance to winning the victory in his spiritual war, then he must say to them a decided No! He dare not beat the air, so sparing himself, his real opponent. Certainly such boxing will never win the prize. Or as Paul, taking farewell of the elders of Ephesus, applied the figure of the race, saying, "I hold not my life of any account as dear unto myself, so that I may accomplish my (race) course, and the ministry which I received from the Lord Jesus, to testify the gospel of the grace of God" (Acts 20: 24).

Obviously Paul is far removed from in any way recommending monasticism or asceticism. Much rather will he say that, as a racer he had to bend all his powers without reserve, including his body and whole outer man, to the one great purpose, to conquer in the battle for holiness and finally to receive in the glory the conqueror's crown from the heavenly Umpire.

3. *Wrestling* (Gk. *palē*) consisted in each combatant exerting himself to throw down the other and pin him to the ground. When picturing the armour of the Christian Paul applies this figure to our conflict with the powers of darkness. Here his picture passes from the realms of sport to military life: "Our wrestling (*palē*) is not against flesh and blood, but against the principalities, against the powers, against the world-rulers of this darkness" (Eph. 6: 12).

This comparison shows how sober and true to life was the apostle's message. Paul knew that the enemy is not to be ignored. He who does not take the powers of darkness seriously will soon be a prey to fanaticism. But fanaticism is very often a near neighbour to grave defeat. It makes us self-secure, deceives us as to the danger, obscures the vision, and weakens moral determination. The enemy, who narrowly observes all this, will attack quite suddenly, and not seldom very severe defeats, even sins of the flesh, are the open evidence of fanaticism and lack of balance.

Therefore Paul says: You must not lose sight of the foe. You are in close contact with him. You have to wrestle with him. He will seek to pin you down. Take seriously his dark reality. Be a wrestler!

But in spite of everything do not despair, for Christ also is present. He is stronger than the foe. Therefore put on the whole armour of God and you will conquer. In this wrestling with the demonic powers the enemy will at last lie on the ground, but you will share the triumph of Christ.

IV. THE RULES OF THE GAMES

1. *Qualifications for entry in the Greek games.* Certain definite conditions were attached to taking part in the contests and gaining the victory. No slaves, but only free men were admitted; no foreigners but only citizens; no impious men nor criminals, but only those without reproach. Freedom, citizenship, and civil honour were indispensable. And naturally bodily strength and practice were required.

For directing the games one or more umpires were chosen (Gk. *agonothetes, athlothetes*). Before these the combatants had to appear to be tested (Gk. *dokimasia*).

Before the contest each individual underwent an often long and special training, which sometimes lasted ten months. To this training there belonged also a general outward sobriety of life. In addition, only such were admitted to the Greek games who had for a certain time practised in a gymnasium.

Before the games started the combatants cast lots as to the order of place. Then they took an oath before the statue of Zeus binding themselves to fight honourably.

Now the Leader gave the signal to begin. A herald stepped out and read the rules of the contests, and called the contestants to enter the lists. A trumpet sounded and the fight began.

This is all symbolical of the Christian warfare, even if a few of these details are not made use of in the figurative speech of the New Testament. For who may enter the arena of faith? Who may run and wrestle, so as to win the victor's crown? Only such as have become *free* from the power of sin, such as are *citizens* of the kingdom of God, and such as set themselves to live in practical *righteousness*.

In I Corinthians Paul calls to mind the self-control and training of the Grecian competitors. In this he sees a picture of the necessity for Christian self-mastery and self-denial. Obviously he thinks here especially of the Isthmian games, held near his Corinthian readers. "Every man that strives in the games is temperate in all things. Now they do it to receive a corruptible crown (wreath); but we an incorruptible. . . . I buffet my body and bring it into bondage (subjection)" (I Cor. 9: 25, 27).

For a victorious Christian life it is a presupposition that we are ready to deny self, to refrain even from lawful things for Christ's sake, to offer spiritual and material sacrifices, to say "No" to self, so as to be able truly to say "Yes" to the Lord. He who is not prepared to sacrifice will not be honoured to gain the crown. He who has regard to his Ego, will one day, when Christ appears, have a great disappointment. He who holds fast to his own convenience, to an earthly mind, to enjoyment of sin, to pride, renders himself unequal to racing. Only serious training in practical holiness, in self-denial, in true discipleship can strengthen spiritual muscle. Only so shall we run and not be weary. Only so shall we be able in the race of faith to hasten from the starting-post to the winning-post. Only so will the heavenly Umpire crown us at last.

At the same time Paul sees a great danger for each preacher of the gospel, even that he may be only a herald, not a racer; one who does indeed read out the rules of the contest, sounds the trumpet, calls others to the conflict, proclaims the start, but does not himself take actual part. Indeed, he reckons with the serious possibility that he himself, the apostle of Christ, may be only a proclaimer but no runner, and therefore also no victor, a caller forth of others but himself not a competitor for the victor's prize.

But in no case and by no means must this be! Never! Therefore he exercised himself in self-control and self-denial: Therefore will he be a runner and a wrestler, so as at last to receive a crown in the day of Jesus Christ.

Have we this same attitude of heart and mind? Let us grasp the situation quite clearly: He only who loses his life for Jesus' sake will win it (John 12: 25; Matt. 16: 25). Christ never sought the favour of the masses (Luke 9: 57-62). He has declared beyond misunderstanding that discipleship is a serious battle, that only they can follow Him really who count the cost and are ready to pay it (Luke 14: 26-33). No battle, no victory; no cross, no crown!

2. *The Regulations of the Games: The Racecourse.* Each combatant was under strict obligation to keep the rules. As regards

the races, including the horse and chariot races, the very lay-out of the construction of the course had been drawn up to make it almost impossible in advance to transgress these laws. It was in particular needful to prevent any racer or runner from gaining an unfair advantage by shortening certain curves. Therefore the track of a circus was skirted for the whole of its length by a wall (Lat. *spina*, backbone). This was adorned with images of the gods, small altars, statues, and towers. At both ends were three pillars (Lat. *metae*) which showed the direction in which to run. In the Circus Maximus to mark the finish there was a mighty obelisk.

At each end of the wall were always seven dolphins or seven bowls (Lat. *ova*, eggs), for the racer, rider or charioteer must cover the course seven times, and as each circuit was made one of the bowls or dolphins was removed, to show the spectators the position of the contest.

At the Circensian games of the Romans, horse and chariot races took a more prominent place than foot-racing. The Emperor Augustus added six-horse chariots to the two- and four-horse (Lat. *biga, quadriga*). There were also chariots drawn by stags. Usually there were 25 races in succession. In each race (Lat. *missus*) there were four teams. The chariots and drivers were distinguished by different colours, white, red, green, and blue. Each had his own supporters among the crowd. Often among these circus parties there came the wildest, fiercest scenes. The Emperor Domitian, the contemporary of the apostle John, added the golden and the purple; but it appears that these lasted only a short time.[1]

3. *Ancient Egyptian Obelisks of Pharaoh Rameses II in the Circus Maximus and the Circus of Nero.* Today the great obelisk of the Circus Maximus stands on one of the most crowded squares in Rome. It is an ancient Egyptian obelisk of Pharaoh Rameses II, of the second millennium B.C. The Emperor Augustus, at vast cost, brought it in a vessel which belonged to him personally, from Heliopolis to Rome (10 B.C.). The vessel was long preserved at Ostia, the port of Rome. In 1688 the obelisk was set up by Pope Sixtus V in the Piazza del Popolo.

There stands today before St. Peter's in Rome the other great

[1] At the end of the third century after Christ, of the four circus parties named after the chief colours, the red and the blue merged, and the white with the green. On this account in the late Roman and Byzantine period they were mostly spoken of as the "Blue" and the "Green."

obelisk that had stood in the circus of Nero. This ancient Egyptian obelisk, which today forms the centre of the wide square before St. Peter's Cathedral, was formerly the centre of that circus which was renowned as the place where Nero prac- tised his barbarities upon the Christians. The writer has seen both obelisks. What thoughts pass through our mind when we stand before such witnesses to ancient and most significant world and church history!

Whoever after rounding the course seven times crossed the starting line even one step, indeed one foot, ahead of the rest carried off the prize.

In all this, however, keep clearly in mind: He only received the prize who had carried through the *full* requirements of the con- test. No relief was allowed. Not the slightest shortening of the course. Only he who had accepted the *whole* contest, with all that was involved, could count on the prospect of being crowned as victor.

Therefore dedicate your life unreservedly to the Lord! Shun no difficulty connected with a holy walk and faithful witness. God never compromises with sin. Therefore also you must never do so. Be ready to perfect a full devotion. Practise sobriety and self-control, deny profit and enjoyment, advantage and convenience so far as these can be a hindrance to your course in the race of faith. Christ gave Himself up entirely for you: therefore must your life be dedicated entirely to Him (John 17: 19).

"The crown worn by King George V at his father's coronation in 1902 bears a tuft of feathers of the ferivah, the rarest species of the bird of paradise. The bird had to be caught and plucked alive, for the feathers lose their lustre immediately after death; as it frequents the haunts of tigers its capture involves great danger; and the Prince of Wales' crown took twenty years to collect. It cost the lives of a dozen hunters. What a wonderful parable of the martyrs' crowns!" (D. M. Panton). And what a wonderful parable of the crowns of all those who have not loved their own life but have consecrated themselves wholly to Christ their Lord! "Be thou faithful unto death, and I will give thee the crown of life" (Rev. 2: 10).

"And if also a man contend in the games, he is not crowned, except he have contended lawfully," that is, according to the rules of the contest (II Tim, 2: 5). Let us remember "that they who run in a race run all, but one receiveth the prize. Even so run that ye may attain" (I Cor. 9: 24). Let us "press on unto perfection" (Heb. 6: 1).

V. THE PRIZE

1. *The Wreaths and Gifts of honour for the Victors.* To be victor in the games was the height of ambition. A city could scarcely have a greater honour than that one of its citizens should be the victor in the great games.

The victor was permitted to erect to himself a statue in the sacred grove at Olympia, and even at Delphi. A number of bases of such statues have been uncovered at Olympia. Banquets were held in the victor's honour. At these feasts songs of celebrated poets were sung. Indeed, such renowned poets as Pindar honoured them in song. Thus an Olympian crown became the pinnacle of human happiness.

At the crowning on the last day the name of the victor was ceremoniously proclaimed by the herald, the name of his father and his country were announced at the same time, and a palm was handed to him.

Great was the honour granted to the victor (Gk. *olympionikes, cf. nike,* victory) when he returned to his native city. He was carried in a chariot with a festive procession. Statues and tablets were erected to him. He was accorded a place of honour on the City Council, and a seat of honour at games and feasts. The victors were free from all State taxes, and enjoyed other notable privileges. Even in later times the thank-offerings, processions, and banquets instituted in their honour were very brilliant.

The prize that beckoned at Olympia was a wreath of olive leaves, at Delphi a laurel wreath, at the Isthmian games a wreath from the fir tree.

The olive twig at Olympia was taken from the sacred wild olive tree near the temple of Zeus in the holiest area of the city. With a golden knife it had been cut by a boy, both of whose parents were alive, and carried to the Umpire in solemn procession.

The twig of laurel of the victor's wreath at Delphi came from the sacred laurel grove of the sun-god Apollo.

2. *Lists of Victors' names.* The names of the victors were recorded. It is reported that Eusebius, the renowned historian of early Christianity, gave a complete list of the victors at Olympia with their homes. This list covered from the beginning of the

Olympiad reckoning (776 B.C.) to the time of the emperor Caracalla
(A.D. 211–217), thus embracing nearly a thousand years.

3. *The Umpire.* The conduct of the games lay in the hands of
judges specially appointed for this (Gk. *hellanodikes*; *cf. Hellas,*
Greece; *dike,* the right). They were also the umpires of the contests. They were distinguished by purple garments.

When the race ended and the name of the victor was announced
by the herald, he had to appear before the raised seat of the
Umpire. From his hand he received the victor's wreath. In
this the judge acted in the name of the god in whose honour the
festival was held.

4. *The famous statue of Zeus in Olympia.* At Olympia it was
Zeus, the king of the gods, who was the proper judge over all
combatants and judges. Therefore at the very start of the games
the wreath was displayed by being set at the foot of his splendid
image on a magnificent table covered with a beautiful cloth.
For the combatants it was "the joy lying before them." And thus
the letter to the Hebrews, applying the figure of the race to Christ
and His people, exhorts us to look unto Jesus, the beginner and
perfecter of faith, who despised shame, and "for the joy lying
before Him" endured the cross, and now sits at the right hand
of the throne of God (Heb. 12: 1, 2).

Olympia was the centre of the worship of Zeus, the king of the
gods. It was in his name that the victor's wreath was granted.
Mighty and imposing was his statue. The greatest Greek
sculptor, Phidias, had created this perfect ideal of Zeus. From
the description of Herodotus it was made of gold and ivory.
Ivory from not less than 300 elephants was used. It was lavishly
adorned with jewels and fine colours. Gilded forms of the
Olympian gods adorned the pedestal. On this pedestal stood the
throne. It likewise was a work of art made of gold, ivory, and
precious stones. On the throne sat Zeus. The colossal statue
was forty feet in height. The countenance of the god expressed
world-ruling power and fatherly mildness.

As a sign of his dignity the left hand held the royal sceptre,
with an eagle at the tip. His garment was a golden robe, full of
folds, which fell around the foot of the throne. It was adorned
with figures of animals and plants, representing the animal and
vegetable kingdoms. The kingdom of metals was represented
by the golden material of the sceptre, the mineral kingdom by the
precious stones. Thus all the kingdoms of nature were shown.

For Zeus is the Lord of the world. All things are through Zeus and in Zeus, who fills the whole creation. "We are also his offspring." "In Zeus we live and move and exist." Thus and similarly, praising Zeus, had the Grecian poets expressed themselves, for example, Aratus of Cilicia, and Kleanthes of Assos (Troas), whom Paul quoted in his speech on Areopagus (Acts 17: 28) [Aratus: *"tou gar kai genos esmen."* Kleanthes: *"ek sou gar genos esmen."*]

In the outstretched right hand of the seated god stood the goddess of victory, Nike (Gk. *nike*, victory), a daughter of Zeus, her figure likewise made of ivory and gold, her wings and robe also of gold. She waited before the god with the victor's crown. For Zeus was the protector of the games and it was he who granted success; therefore Nike had the victor's wreath in her hand, to be handed to the winner in the name of the god.

5. *Five wreaths (crowns) of victory as mentioned in the New Testament.* Is not the whole an astonishing, many-sided picture of the race and completion of the spiritual life? The arena of faith, the training, the self-control, the ruthless denial of self, the herald, the entrance to the racecourse, the different kinds of contests, the racing to the goal, the boxing, the wrestling, the rules of the combats, Christ the Umpire, the danger of being disqualified, the appearing of the victor before the exalted throne of the divine Judge on the great coming day of the distribution of prizes! It is out of His hand the victors will receive the wreath and palm. The lists of the victors ("book of life"), the triumphal entry in the homeland, the banquet, the festival, the gifts, the place of honour—in fact, scarcely one essential feature of the whole course of the games has escaped the writers of the New Testament and not been employed in their figurative speech.

In the British Museum in London the writer saw the tablet from the theatre at Ephesus of a combatant of the second century after Christ. The inscription runs: "He *fought* three *fights* (Gk. *egonisato agonas*) and was twice *crowned with wreaths* (Gk. *estephthe*; verbum *stepho*, poetical form of *stephanoō*)." Doubtless such inscriptions were known to Paul, and at the close of his service, as he reviews his "course" (Gk. *dromos*), what does he say? "I have *fought* the good *fight* (Gk. *agona egonismai*) . . . henceforth there is laid up for me the *wreath* (Gk. *stephanos*) of righteousness" (II Tim. 4: 7).[1]

[1] Inscription at Ephesus: *egonisato agonas treis estephthe dyo.* Paul's word in II Tim. 4: 7 : *ton kalon agona egonismai . . . loipon apokeitai moi ho tes dikaiosynes stephanos.*

This wreath is unfading and imperishable (I Cor. 9: 25).
Christ our Lord is the righteous Umpire. Therefore the allotting
of the wreaths will be just. Only those, however, who pass the
test will receive the victor's prize (Rev. 2: 10).

How manifold are the forms in the pictorial language of the
New Testament which describe the glorification of the victors.
To be exact one must say "garland (wreath)" rather than "crown"
(Gk. *stephanos*). The faithful will be garlanded:

The Victorious Fighter
   with the wreath of righteousness (II Tim. 4: 8);
The Steadfast Runner
   with the unfading wreath (I Cor. 9: 25, 26);
The One Faithful unto Death
   with the wreath of life (Rev. 2: 10; Jas. 1: 12);
The Unselfish Labourer
   with the wreath of honour (I Thess. 2: 19; Phil. 4: 1);
The Example to the Flock
   with the wreath of glory (I Pet. 5: 3, 4).

At times the comparisons pass from the athletic world to the
military. The reasons for this can be easily understood. In
Ephesians 6 Paul uses the sport figure from wrestling (*palē*) in his
description of the Christian's armour, and thus in a section which
takes its chief comparisons from military life (vv. 10–20):
"our wrestling (*palē*) is not against flesh and blood, but against
the principalities, against the powers, against the world-rulers
of this darkness" (v. 12). Likewise it is quite possible that also
in some other places the picture of the victor's wreath taken from
the athletic world, refers at the same time to military life. For
Roman soldiers as well the decorations consisted for the more
part of wreaths (garlands). There were diverse wreaths for
different heroic deeds: one sort of wreath for the soldier who
saved the life of another; another kind of wreath for him who first
stormed into an enemy fort; yet another form of wreath for an
act of exceptional bravery which saved the fatherland.

In I Peter the picture of the "wreath of glory" quite apparently
comes from country life. There the apostle encourages the
elders in the church to self-denying service as shepherds. He
names Christ the "Chief Shepherd." When Christ shall appear
they will receive the eternal glory as reward for their faithful
service as shepherds: "When the chief Shepherd shall be manifested ye shall receive the wreath of glory that fadeth not away"

(I Pet. 5: 4).   Here also in the original the term *stephanos* denotes garland (wreath), not crown.   This is shown not only by the context ("shepherd, flock") which evidently points to simple country life, but also by the addition "that fadeth not away," does not wither.   For no metal crown can wither, only a wreath of flowers, leaves, or twigs.   The picture the apostle employs is not of a sparkling diadem of gold and jewels, but of a simple wreath, living, beautiful, remaining in freshness for ever.

6.   *The White Stone in the letter to Pergamum.*   Another reference to athletic contests lies at the base of the promise to the overcomers in the church at Pergamum: "To him that overcometh . . . will I give a white stone, and upon the stone a new name written, which no one knoweth but he that receiveth it" (Rev. 2: 17).

This promise is understood differently.   We mention two explanations.

One refers to a custom of voting in ancient legal practice, which must have been used in Pergamum.   A Roman High Court sat in this city.   In Greco-Roman antiquity various black or white stones were used for arriving at the final verdict of guilty or not-guilty.   The judges who wished to acquit the accused placed in an urn a white stone; those who would condemn him placed a black stone.   In the light of this custom the promise of the Lord would mean: "Ye Christian witnesses in Pergamum: you have to go through much reproach and contempt.   Men blaspheme your faith.   They slander your good name.   But be confident that though the whole world may enter your name in the black register, may all unitedly give a black stone, I, the chief Judge of the universe, the Lord of all, declare Myself *for* you: I shall give you a white stone.   Therefore be sure of victory; the Supreme Court is on your side!"   Or, as Paul testifies, "If God be for us, who can be against us?" (Rom. 8: 31).

In this explanation, however, a difficulty remains unsolved. In Roman legal procedure these stones were never inscribed with a name.   They were simply smooth stones, black or white, or small clay tablets, dark or clear.   But the promise deals with a stone on which a *name* is written, and the name of a *victor*.   Moreover, this white stone is not placed in an urn, but *given to the victor personally*, and this on the *day of perfecting*, the great coming day of glory.

The other explanation, which is certainly right, refers to a custom of the Greek games. The victor's prize at the games was not only garlands of olive, wreaths of laurel, or palm sprays, but also of objects of value and gifts of gold; indeed, at times gifts continued for life. According to Plutarch, as early as the fourth century B.C., Solon, the lawgiver of Athens, had ordered that to the victor in the Isthmian games should be given 100 drachmas, and in the Olympian games 500 (one drachma = 1s. 6d.). This made necessary that the Leader of the games (*agonothetes*) should give to the home-going victor a certificate of his victory. Corresponding to the festal occasion this took a durable and artistic form. It was a small tablet of white stone in which the name of the victor was inscribed by an expert carver.

The promise to the overcomer attaches to this custom. Here we have in fact the white stone, and on it a name written, the name of the overcomer, and this stone is given to the victor himself, and all this is to take place in the coming day of glory when he enters his eternal home after having conquered in the racecourse.

Thus this picture of the "white stone" with the victor's name declares that the combatant will be acknowledged by the Lord as a conqueror. The despised and persecuted will attain to honour. The sentence of rejection by man will be reversed, and those here hated and expelled will be granted heavenly riches and eternal glory. In the race for the prize faith wins the victory.

And as regards the names of the believers, despised and dishonoured for the sake of their testimony to Christ, let them know that the Lord will give them a *new* name, holy and noble, a name of honour, which answers to the greatness of the triumph and the brightness of the glory: "And the nations shall see thy righteousness, and all the kings thy glory: and thou shalt be called by a new name, which the mouth of the Lord shall name. Thou shalt also be a crown of beauty in the hand of the Lord, and a royal diadem in the hand of thy God . . . for the Lord delighteth in thee" (Isa. 62: 2–4; 65: 15).

At the same time the honouring of the runner will correspond to his individual relationship to Christ. Each will receive a new name which "no one knows save he who receives it." Each has his particular history. God is not only God of the community but also of the individual. There exists a mysterious bond which binds the redeemed soul to Christ, the Redeemer. Each soul has its own "most holy place," to which only the Lord has access. Therefore, in the perfecting, each member of the church will be in a fellowship with Christ which no other will share in the same manner, and which therefore no other will fully perceive. However inward and deep is the union of the members with each other, yet no one of them will receive in the glory his new name through the mediation and channel of another member, but each only directly from the Head; so much so that each has his own portion in Christ, his own gift, his own calling, which belong to him alone. Thus the church of the overcomers will retain its inexhaustible manifoldness, through which it will reveal the riches of the Divine grace.

The great basic law of individuality shall be fully displayed in the glory. Each victor will receive a name which is granted to him alone, which will fully and clearly express his personal characteristics, his special relation to Christ, and his special calling in the service of God. There will be no extinguishing of the personality, no submergence in the mass, no kind of Nirvana in which the individual billow melts away into the ocean flood. No; God intends character!—an organism of distinguishable personalities; men with a "Thou and I" relationship with Himself, who in the great "We" of the organic kingdom of God possess a transfigured, holy "I." Therefore can each praise Him for the particular relationship of love which He has to *him*, for the wonderful ways which He has taken with *him*.

> Yet each his own sweet harp will bring,
> And his own special song will sing. (*Gerhard Tersteegen*).

7. *The peril of being disqualified.* But with all this we must not forget that the entrance upon the race does not guarantee the prize. The garland is not given at the beginning but only at the end of the race. It will be bestowed on those only who have contended according to the rules of the contest and have gained the victory.

Without doubt salvation and eternal life are free gifts of the grace of God, granted to faith on the basis of the sacrifice of Golgotha. But the degree of glory, the victor's garland, is according to the faithfulness of the believer. The Scripture everywhere gives solemn warning to this effect: "Hold fast that which thou hast, that no one take thy crown" (wreath: Rev. 3: 11): "If a man contend in the games, he is not crowned, except he have contended lawfully" (II Tim. 2: 5). Therefore let us take to heart the questions put forward by a man of God of today

E

in view of the five victor's wreaths which the New Testament promises to the overcomer.

The Wreath of Incorruption—

"In a race all run, but *one* receiveth the prize ... Now they do it to receive a corruptible wreath; but we an incorruptible" (I Cor. 9: 24, 25).

Can the racer be crowned who failed in running?

The Wreath of Rejoicing—

"What is our hope or joy, or wreath of glorying? Are not even ye before our Lord Jesus at His coming?" (I Thes. 2: 19).

Can he be crowned for turning many to righteousness (Dan. 12: 3) who never turned one?

The Wreath of Glory—

"The elders therefore among you I exhort. ... Tend the flock of God ... and when the chief shepherd shall be manifested ye shall receive the wreath of glory" (I Pet. 5: 1–4).

Can a disciple be rewarded for shepherding the flock of God who never did it?

The Wreath of Righteousness—

"I have kept the faith: *henceforth* there is laid up for me the wreath of righteousness ... and not to me only, but also to all them that have *loved His appearing*" (II Tim. 4: 7, 8).

Can the wreath of watchfulness be given to him who never watched?

The Wreath of Life—

"Blessed is the man that endureth temptation: for *when he hath been approved*, he shall receive the wreath of life" (Jas. 1: 12).

Can he be crowned for resisting temptation who succumbed to it?

"When Roumania became a kingdom in 1881, King Charles, as there was no crown, said: Send to the arsenal and melt an iron crown out of the captured cannon, in token that it was won on the field of battle, and bought and paid for with our lives" (D. M. Panton).

8. *The Heavenly Glory.* Christ will grant to the victors eternal glory. They will see the king in His beauty. They will reign with Him for ever. They will worship Him as His priests in the heavenly sanctuary. They will radiate brightness as the stars in the kingdom of their Father.

As regards the *majesty* of God,
    their portion will be holy *worship*.
As regards the *nature* of God,
    His *image* will be perfectly revealed in them.
As regards the *life* of God,
    their *sonship* will be made manifest in glory.
As regards the *creation* of God,
    they will *rule* over the universe for ever.

"He that overcometh, I will give to him to sit down with Me in My throne, as I also overcame, and sat down with My Father in His throne" (Rev. 3: 21).

This is the full content of the victor's prize. It is the inheritance, incorruptible, undefiled, unfading, which by God's power is reserved in heaven for faith to attain (I Pet. 1: 4). As yet we live here below in weakness and imperfection: "It is not yet made manifest what we shall be." But: "We know that, if He shall be manifested, we shall be like Him; for we shall see Him even as He is" (I John 3: 2). And "when Christ, who is our life, shall be manifested, then shall ye also with Him be manifested in glory" (Col. 3: 4). "Having therefore these promises, beloved, let us cleanse ourselves from all defilement of flesh and spirit, perfecting holiness in the fear of God" (II Cor. 7: 1). "And every one that hath this hope set on Him purifieth himself, even as He is pure" (I John 3: 3).

CHAPTER IV

THE RACE THAT IS SET BEFORE US

"Therefore let us also seeing we are compassed about with so great a cloud of witnesses, lay aside every weight, and the sin which doth so easily beset us, and let us run with patience the race that is set before us, looking unto Jesus the author and perfecter of faith; who for the joy that was set before him endured the cross, despising shame, and hath sat down at the right hand of the throne of God.

For consider him that hath endured such gainsaying of sinners against himself, that ye wax not weary, fainting in your souls" (Heb. 12: 1–3).

THE whole gospel is full of life. Its source is God the Living One. Its mediator is Christ the Risen One. Its power is the Spirit of God, "the Spirit that maketh alive."

For this reason God's salvation is not something which has only historically happened and was completed in the past, but it is a continual process. It is not a present received once and for all, but a giving which increasingly presents us with something more. Every grace is a vital dynamic action given to us by God in Christ through the Holy Spirit. There is nothing static but everything is dynamic. There is no standing still but a marching forward, no looking aside or backward, but a striving towards the goal. Everything is alive and active, a spiritual working, a holy motion, pulsated and animated by "waves" produced by Spirit-wrought heavenly powers.

God's gifts are not like an anchor which holds the ship of our life firm, but they are rather to be compared with the sails of a ship into which the wind of the Spirit of God can blow mightily, thus carrying the boat forward.

I. THE "APPOINTMENT" OF THE RACE

The author of the Hebrews letter declares that we should run with patience the race "that is set before us" (Heb. 12: 1). This does not only mean the race as lying before us from the view-point of time or, so to speak, space. What is meant is something dynamic. The race (Gk. *agon*) is "set before us" as our *task*. It is our *duty* to run. The race is God-appointed (Gk. *prokeimenon*). The phrase *Prokeitai agon!* (Lat. *Propositum est certamen*), "The battle lieth before!" was the usual Greek (answering to the Latin) expression for the race which was to be run, and which was publicly announced by a crier, together with the rules of the race and the prize.

You cannot separate your own personal life of faith from being a runner in a race. God has appointed that you should *run*. True sanctification can be experienced practically only in a life of a Spirit-energized dynamic effort, and this effort involves our whole being, spirit, soul, and body. He who will not run in the race has from the very start abandoned the crown and the prize of victory. And as Satan, the great adversary, never admits being beaten until his final overthrow (Rev. 20: 10), the battle and the race will never end for us until we have reached the goal of our course.

This means that you must take your personal responsibility very seriously. You must reckon in confident faith with the victorious powers of Christ the Saviour. But on the other hand do not overlook the reality of the enemy. Weigh seriously all the paralysing powers which emanate from him. Concentrate on the goal. Live in the holy energy of a consecrated life. We can never make peace with sin. Never forget that a real life of faith means a running in the race. Remember: "And if also a man contend in the games, he is not crowned, except he have contended lawfully" (II Tim. 2: 5). The new birth is not the finishing-post but the starting-post. If you would reach the finishing-post, you must *run*.

The race is a very serious affair. Demons surround us. Powers of darkness block our way. And these powers are not only around us but endeavour to work in us (Eph. 6: 12). Let us therefore be hard on ourselves. Let us bring our own bodies into subjection (I Cor. 9: 27). Let us control our own souls. Let us concentrate and fix our spiritual eyes on Jesus Christ. Only those who strive will be crowned. Only victors will be exalted. Christ Himself says: "To him that *overcometh* will I grant to sit with me in my throne" (Rev. 3: 21).

What is the background of this battle? Our answer is as follows:

1. We must be warriors because the whole universe is involved in a mighty revolution, the mightiest indeed, which has ever taken place—it is the battle between Satan and God; and because, according to the testimony of the whole Scripture, the central battle area of this conflict is this our earth, the habitation of mankind, so that here the decision will be reached. This is the *cosmological and super-historical* background of our conflict.

2. We must be warriors because, although Christ by His death and His resurrection has won the victory fundamentally, yet historically the full practical outworking of this His victory has not yet been secured. Thus, in the development of God's redemptive plan, our present dispensation lies in the tension between the hiddenness of the kingdom of God and the openness of the rule of Satan. This is the *dispensational* background of our battle situation.

3. We must be warriors because it necessarily corresponds to the combined divine and human character of the kingdom of God to allow the creature freedom of will. So that the one who has been called to the kingdom has not only to decide at his *conversion* which master he will serve but has thereupon to make the same decision every day and in each practical detail of his life of *sanctification*. This is the *moral* and *dynamic* background of our conflict.

For these three main reasons the race is God-appointed.

II. The Attitude which is Necessary to Reach the Goal

What attitude of mind must we have if we wish to win the race? A poet has rightly said:

> To fight is not enough alone;
> 'Tis only victors mount the throne!

In order to be a conqueror a very definite spiritual attitude of faith is required. The author of the Hebrews letter gives us four main points of view:

1. *Looking to the Victor.* He who would be victorious must look to Christ. "Let us look unto Jesus." The battle which He fought out on Golgotha is at the same time our example for our own personal battle. His victory is the foundation for our

victory. The remarkable thing about the battle of faith is that we do not properly have to *strive* for the victory but that we *possess* it already. We have the victory in Christ, our Forerunner, our Conqueror. Therefore we do not have to battle *for* the victory but we can fight *from* the victory He has won. For this reason we can live out of His fulness. In Christ is opened unto us an everlasting source of riches. Joy in Him is our strength to conquer.

It was during the first world war. In the German cities was every kind of suffering and need. Many housewives had great difficulty in giving their loved ones enough food from the small rations obtainable. One day a simple woman arrived at the seaside from a north German city. It was the first time in her life that she had been able to enjoy a sight of the vast ocean. She was quite overwhelmed with the magnificence of the view and with the endless waters. In her astonishment she cried out: "At last after all something which they cannot ration!"

We smile at this woman. And yet one can understand her when one considers her circumstances. But the inexhaustible heavenly resources are a thousand times greater, and these the Lord in His grace has placed at the disposal of His children. Here we find truly a fulness which exceeds all earthly measure, riches which God does not distribute in small portions but in mighty overflowing heavenly gifts. God's children are royal children, for which reason they should live royally by enjoying these spiritual riches in their life of faith. Their heavenly Father proves Himself to be a generous royal Giver in all His blessings.

About thirty years ago I took part in a Christian Conference in Northern England and have never forgotten a short Bible exegesis which one of the speakers gave. He spoke of the fulness which is opened up in Christ from the "unsearchable riches" of His heavenly blessings (Eph. 3: 8), of Christ Himself, the "unspeakable gift" of God (II Cor. 9: 15). And then he pointed to two small and yet very significant words in the Ephesian letter, the words "according to." "For this cause I bow my knees unto the Father . . . that He would grant you, *according to* the riches of His glory, to be strengthened with power through His Spirit in the inward man" (Eph. 3: 14, 16). And then he spoke as follows: The expression "*according to* the riches of His glory" conveys very much more than if the writer had only said: "*out of* His riches." If a beggar were to meet a millionaire in the street and if the latter were to give him at his request, shall we say,

a sixpence, then we should be able to say perfectly correctly that
he had given him "out of" his riches. But nobody would think
of saying that he had given him "according to" his riches. If
he had given him "according to" his millions, the gift would
have been very different.

How does our God act? Does He only give us "out of" His
riches? Here a little joy and there a little victory? Today a
little help and tomorrow perhaps an occasional answer to prayer?
No, He the all-sufficient One gives "according to" His riches.
His standard is not our daily needs—even though if this only were
the case that would make us very happy: "As thy days so shall
thy strength be" (Deut. 33: 25), but He uses the measure and
criterion of eternity for our temporal needs and gives us His
blessings "according to" His fulness.

This is the reason why the word "abound" is one of Paul's
favourite expressions (Gk. *perisseuein*). He speaks of abounding
faith (II Cor. 8: 7), of abounding love (II Thess. 1: 3), abounding
liberality (II Cor. 8: 2), abounding diligence and knowledge
(II Cor. 8: 7), abounding hope (Rom. 15: 13).

Another word which he uses again and again is the word
hyper = super.

The apostle has a tendency to build up words using "super"
(Gk. *hyper*) and he does it so often that this is one of the characteristics of his literary style. Of a total of 29 combinations
using the word "super" which occur in the whole New Testament no less than 19 belong to him alone and 4 are shared with
other biblical authors.

Thus he speaks of

a "*super*"-growth in faith (II Thess. 1, 3).[1]
a "*super*"-victory and conquest (Rom. 8: 37).[2]
a "*super*"-exceeding grace of God (II Cor. 9: 14).[3]
a "*super*"-fulness of riches (Eph. 2: 7).[4]
a "*super*"-exceeding greatness of His power (Eph. 1: 19).[5]
a "*super*"-exceeding glory (II Cor. 3: 10).[6]

Furthermore he speaks of

---

[1] *hyper*-auxanei he pistis.
[2] *hyper*-nikomen, we "hyper" overcome.
[3] dia tēn *hyper*-ballousan charin.
[4] *hyper*-ballon ploutos.
[5] *hyper*-ballon megethos tēs dynameos.
[6] heineken tēs *hyper*-ballouses doxes

a knowledge of a "*super*"-exceeding love of Christ (Eph. 3: 19).[1]

a peace in Christ which "*super*"-exceeds all understanding (Phil. 4: 7).[2]

a "*super*"-excelling joy even in tribulation (II Cor. 7: 4).[3]

The foundation of this is however

the "*super*"-exaltation of Jesus (Phil. 2: 9).[4]

the exceeding "*super*"-abundant presence of grace (I Tim. 1: 14).[5]

the "*super*"-abounding of grace just where sin had formerly "abounded" (Rom. 5: 20).[6]

"Therefore, my beloved brethren, be ye steadfast, unmoveable, always abounding in the work of the Lord, for as much as ye know that your labour is not vain in the Lord" (I Cor. 15: 58).

Astounding, indeed, is the fulness which the apostle describes in II Cor. 9: 8 in a very few words, in fact in a sentence of less than four lines: "God is able to make *all* grace abound unto you; that ye, having *always all* sufficiency, in *all* things, may abound unto every (= *all*) good work."[7]

In Christ is not only a full measure but a "super"-full measure of divine all-sufficiency. His giving more than meets the needs of our daily life. Therefore we do not need to worry ourselves miserably in everyday life but we have the right to be victors in Him, yea to be more than conquerors, to be "super-conquerors in Him" (Rom. 8: 37).

In the benediction of the second prayer in the Ephesian letter the apostle combines these his two favourite words "abounding" (Gk. *perisseuein*) and "*super*" (*hyper*) and thus coins a new word which he then *further* strengthens by the addition of a second word (Gk. *ek*): "Now unto Him that is able to do *exceedingly abundantly above* (Gk. *hyper-ek-perissou*) all that we ask or think . . . unto Him be glory in the church and in Christ Jesus unto all the ages Amen" (Eph. 3: 20). We can perhaps come closest to the surprisingly rich and deep meaning of the Greek word by translating: "Exceeding abundantly more" or: "Far beyond all measure

[1] tēn *hyper*-ballousan tēs gnoseos agapen tou Christou.

[2] he eirene . . . he *hyper*-echousa panta noun.

[3] *hyper*-perisseumai te chara.

[4] ho theos auton *hyper*-hypsosen.

[5] *hyper*-pleonasen de he charis.

[6] *hyper*-perisseusen he charis.

[7] Greek pasan, panti, pantote, pasan, pan.

more," "More than overflowingly," "Far beyond all that we need, and even then exceeding abundantly more than that."

God does not merely wish to fill the vessel of your life up to the brim. He does not only even pour in His fulness of blessing so that it just comes to overflowing. No, even the word "overflowing" is not adequate. God makes us to "more than overflow." Such a "super-mighty" redemption is given us in Christ.

And now, my reader, place your own experience against these God-given possibilities. Must we not humble ourselves before the Lord—you and I—and be ashamed of ourselves that we have drunken so little from these fountains? How often we are like a foolish beggar who should stand before a wealthy benefactor begging for gifts which this generous man had already offered and held out to him! And yet at the same time this beggar complains of his misery, bewails his poverty, begs and begs, but does not stretch out his hand to take the gift which has been long proffered him, in fact immediately after he had begun to beg! So the bewailer continues bewailing and the giver remains the profferer; but in spite of all the begging on the one side and the willingness to give on the other side the situation remains unchanged. How different the situation would be if we adopted the attitude of faith: "And if we know that He heareth us, whatsoever we ask, we know that we *have* the petitions which we have asked of Him" (I John 5: 15). But this can be experienced only by looking unto Christ in genuine faith.

"Let us look unto Jesus!"

The moment however we look away from Christ our experience of His fulness ceases. There is no power to overcome. Things become important for us which, seen in the light of eternity, are of no consequence. Then the deceiving power of sin bewitches us. And if, in our opinion, we are not properly honoured or respected, if our own self-will, our desire to possess, our own presumed importance does not receive satisfaction enough, then we slip into sin. We are easily hurt, become loveless, are filled with an earthly mind, or become fretful and anxious. We have lost our sense of proportion because of not looking unto Christ. The centre of gravity has been changed and is no longer in God but in ourselves. We have lost our way because we have lost our sense of direction in Christ.

In this condition only one thing can help us: Looking afresh to Jesus Christ. Repentance and humiliation before Him and then continuing steadfastly to keep our eyes upon Him. This purifies and restores us, and only this attitude of mind brings with it growth in grace and blessed happy sanctification.

In a West European city there was once a royal visit and the streets were lined with crowds of people. In the foremost line, waiting to see the royal visitor, stood a mother and her little boy. At last the royal guest arrived, and with him the pomp of his court, and drove by. Everything happened relatively quickly. Suddenly the young mother stretched out her arm and enthusiastically pointed to the king as he drove by, so that her little boy should see him. And with a loud voice she cried: "*Look at him and never forget it all your life!*"

How do we act in respect of Christ, the King of all kings? Let us take for our motto in life: "Look at Him and never forget it all your life!" Let us look unto Jesus! He is our salvation, our helper, our example, our strength.

2. *Looking to the comrades in arena.* The author of the Hebrews letter founds his admonition: "Let us . . . run the race" on the example of the heroes of faith in the Old Testament. "Wherefore seeing we also are compassed about with so great a cloud of witnesses . . . let us run" (Heb. 12: 1). This means: "Ye witnesses of Jesus Christ in these New Testament times of the church, look back into the history of the Old Testament. Think of all that has been endured, suffered, and fought for: think also of the victories. Always, at all times, there have been heroes of faith. Ye are not alone. Ye are not the first to have suffered for the truth.

This is the real meaning of Hebrews 11, this mighty and imposing chapter on the victors of faith. If we had to invent a title for this chapter to express that which the author of the letter obviously wishes, we could think of no better one than the three short words: "*Faith is able.*" Hebrews 11 is nothing less than a proof from practical experience, covering more than four millenniums, that men and women of all times, in various lands, in all positions, exalted and humble, in the most varied situations, in war and peace, have been able to stand the test and prove the reality that living faith is the power of God. This however means at the same time that what others have been able to do, you also can do. Your God is not only a God of yesterday but the very God of today. *Your* God.

And if Hebrews 11 introduces such a *long* list of heroes of faith, this is done in order to give the proof that true faith has not only been exercised in exceptional times of revival or a relatively short period, but also in the long periods between these special times of blessing. In fact it is a power giving spiritual victory at all times, in fact in *your* times, in *your* life and *my* life, in *your* circumstances and all *your* trials and testings, so that there is no excuse if you fail.

Thus looking to our fellow-runners brings us encouragement and at the same time a deep consciousness of our responsibility. "Wherefore seeing we also are compassed about with so great a cloud of witnesses . . . let us *run*!"

When it is pointed out that this large number of men and women of faith "compasses us about" (Gk. *perikeimenon*), and when they are compared with a thick "cloud" of witnesses, it is intended that their large number should be emphasized. Just as the historical frame of more than forty long and weary centuries during which these battles of faith were fought should serve to emphasize the *time* factor, so the expressions "compassing about" and "cloud" should emphasize the great *number* of these heroes of faith and this at the same time, so to speak, under the view-point of spiritual "space" and region. Wherever you look you will see witnesses of faith. They "compass" you about. That, however, means you are encouraged from all sides. You are actually surrounded by irrefutable proofs that true faith never fails.

The expression "witness" scarcely means that these men of God are "spectators," from a position outside the earth and its affairs, of our present race and strife. It is not as though they watch from their exalted seats the battle in the "arena" here below. There are no scriptures which tell us that those who have left this earthly life take an active conscious part in the things concerning the church militant. They are characterized here as people who gave witness in their generation, and who, when we examine their life, are an example for us today of "faith in action" winning victories in God. Although death has taken them away from this scene, their testimony remains. So that by this means and in this sense these heroes of faith of yesterday are, as it were, present with us today. In fact, they "compass us about" and encourage us in the faith.

Finally, the high dignity of all active service and sacrifice for Christ is thus brought into its true Biblical light. The witnesses of faith of the present are thus brought together with the witnesses of the past, which, so to say, raises the confessors of the present to the peerage attained by the prophets of the past. They are made members of the great army of God's heroes, of those who bear God's highest honours and whom God Himself confesses (Heb. 11: 16). They are people who indeed went through shame and who were despised, but of whom, of a truth, the earth is not worthy (Heb. 11: 38). And this, too, is a reason why we should take courage, even though the doings of our personal life are incomparably smaller and most unimportant compared with these heroes, and even though our service and witness, and the whole frame of our life, according to the appointment and the leading of God, is but very humble.

3. *Looking to the enemy.* In all this the Bible is exceedingly sober. It nowhere favours unhealthy eccentricity. For this reason the Scriptures speak quite honestly of the opposing enemy forces which stand in the way of the race of faith. The Scriptures never utter things which one sometimes hears from fanatical over-spirituality, such as "You do not need to fight against sin any more. Only look to Christ alone. Then all will be well." Not at all, in fact, just the opposite. Perfectly clearly and in detail the Scriptures warn us that "our wrestling is not against flesh and blood, but against principalities, against the powers, against the world-rulers of this darkness, against the spiritual hosts of wickedness in the heavenly places" (Eph. 6: 12). The Bible directs our attention to *both* sides: to the victor and to the enemy, to heaven and to hell, to Christ, Who gives us all things, and to Satan who denies and opposes all things intended for our good.

But with all our faith in Christ we should not think too lightly of the power of the enemy. He is a sombre reality who would interfere forcibly in our life. Without question, the enemy is great. But thanks be to God, Christ, the Victor, is greater. Luther was right in saying of the "ancient foe":

> The ancient prince of hell
> Hath risen with purpose fell;
> Strong mail of craft and power
> He weareth in this hour;
> On earth is not his fellow.

But he was just as right when he triumphantly added:

> With force of arms we nothing can
> Full soon were we down-ridden;
> *But for us fights the proper Man*
> *Whom God himself hath bidden.*
> Ask ye, Who is this same?
> Christ Jesus is his name,
> The Lord Sabaoth's Son;
> He, and no other one
>   Shall conquer in the battle!
> (translated by *Thomas Carlyle*).

This state of war will continue until the fulness of the times. For the "flesh" is a rebel. It is not subject to the law of God (Rom. 8: 7). It even makes the law of God "weak" and ineffective (Rom. 8: 3). It never will die here below. It cannot be sanctified but must be overcome in strenuous conflict, in the battle of faith. "For the flesh lusteth against the Spirit, and the Spirit against the flesh" (Gal. 5: 17). Thus power is opposed to power, will to will, and lust to lust. And this insurgent against the will of God will never capitulate in his rebellion. He is like a spiral which at once springs up when the pressure resting upon it is taken away. He is like the woman in the "ephah," the "wickedness" of which the prophet Zechariah writes in his night-visions. The moment the weight of lead was removed from the mouth of the ephah she sprang out and exposed herself and could only be cast back into the ephah by force (Zech. 5: 6–11). The wicked one is like a captive revolutionary in the Christian who only waits for the moment when he can escape his prison and who has sharp eyes to search out every imaginable opportunity to get out.

Therefore resist sin from the beginning. Never play with sin. To be tempted by sin is indeed not yet sin itself. Thinking of evil things is not the same as "evil thoughts." But in no case must we permit sin to find a lodging in our mind. Learn to say "no" right in the moment sin approaches you. Only thus is victory possible. Think of the truth of the proverb: Sow a thought, reap a deed: sow a deed, reap a habit: sow a habit, reap character: sow character, reap destiny.

The spiritual mind is always on the watch, for it knows the dangers and watches and prays. The spiritual mind knows that our way is not a bed of roses but an arena, a racecourse. The full victory is yet future. We do not dwell at the moment in Immanuel's land but in a foreign country. We are strivers, fighters, wanderers who are hurrying away. We have been brought into a holy movement. Our Christian life is a "way" (Acts 9: 2; 18: 26; 19: 9), a course which we have to run. We are on a pilgrimage to the heavenly Jerusalem in "Christian's armour."

Three hostile powers can hinder us in the race of faith: the world, sins, and burdensome weights.

> The "world" with her contradiction,
> "Sin" with her power to entice,
> "Burdens" with their paralysing pressure.

The world hated Christ. Her "contradiction" brought Him to the cross. As Christ's disciples we should therefore expect to be rejected. Intimate friendship with unbelievers, marriage between converted and unconverted, striving after earthly goods or to attain recognition and human honours at the cost of a clear confession of Christ—all this may indeed lessen the contrast between the world and Christ's followers, but at the same time it makes it impossible for us to be real "runners" in the race. In the end every one who compromises is in a serious measure a loser. He will never reach the goal and will never be crowned (II Tim. 2: 5).

Sin strives to encircle us from all sides. Its strategy of war is exceedingly skilful. The Hebrews letter uses a very impressive word saying that sin is completely enclosing us (lit. standing well around us from all sides, Gk. *eu-peri-statos*).

It is as though the runner finds himself in a crowd of people and must clear himself a way before he can run. Sin blocks the way for us inwardly and outwardly, and if we are not to be brought to a stop it requires a manly and earnest effort. It is possible that the author when using the expression "sin being around" thinks of the long heavy robe which would have to be laid aside if the runner is to run unhindered. This would also fit into the context. In any case the sense is the following:

Sin wishes cunningly to encompass and to lay siege to us. It attacks us concentratedly from all sides, tries to effect a kind of military "encircling movement," and is exceedingly skilful. The Greek word *peri-istamai*, which is etymologically related to the word *eu-peri-statos*, which the writer of the Hebrews letter uses

here for "beset," is, as Professor Franz Delitzsch remarks, a
common military word used in war, sieges, and in hunting,
meaning "to encompass."

Sin has two chief methods of procedure:

It pretends to be the "generous friend" and promises gain or
at least the prevention of a loss, a pleasure or at least the possibility of avoiding a difficulty. It offers an advantage or at least
the lessening of an inconvenience. Sin uses sensuousness,
tyranny, avarice, or "white" lies. Sin is able to adopt ever new
forms and to transform itself with regard to its tactics in a remarkable manner. It can completely camouflage itself and can even
deny the existence of its own master, Satan. "The gate of hell
is decked with garlands." If this were not the case no man
would be seduced to sin. The Wicked One clothes himself in
the clothing of something "useful" or "good." Every lie lives
from a certain element of truth which is in fact contained in it and
which it misuses. A *mere* lie, that is a lie which is *only* a lie,
cannot exist.

The second method of procedure used by sin tactically is
the following. Before the deed has been done its wickedness is
minimized. Afterwards however it is *magnified* so as to rob us of
our courage in order that we may lose hope that we can ever
again become pure and free. "My sin is greater than can be for-
given me" (Gen. 4: 13 lit.). So sin deceives us first of all into
frivolity and then into melancholic depression. Its aim is to
make us give up the battle so that we may serve it in worldliness
and slavery. Thus it is first of all a friend and then a tyrant,
first a liberator (Psa. 2: 3) and then a jailor, first of all it dazzles
us and then surrounds us with darkness. These are its tactics
in "cunningly encircling us."

But what a strong encouragement! There is a still greater
power which surrounds us! This power is God and the power
of His salvation. Although it is true that sin is always ready to
attack and is most skilful in lurking in most unlikely places and
surrounding us from all sides, that is even more true which the
psalmist exultantly confesses of his Saviour God: "Thou shalt
compass me about with songs of deliverance" (Psa. 32: 7). It
is a fact:

He, the Lord our God, is "*round about* His people" (Psa. 125:
2). The name of the Lord is a strong tower (Prov. 18: 10).
The redeemed are kept safe therein.

The Lord our God rules *over* us in perfect love. "As an

eagle that stirreth up her nest, that fluttereth over her young,
the Lord alone did lead him" (Deut. 32: 11–12).

The Lord our God protects us from *below*, that we may not
fall; for: "The eternal God is thy dwelling place, and underneath
are the everlasting arms" (Deut. 33: 27). "He bare them on His
pinions" (Deut. 32: 11).

The Lord our God is by our *side*. "I have set the Lord always
before me: because He is at my right hand, I shall not be moved"
(Psa. 16: 8). "A thousand shall fall at thy side, and ten thousand
at thy right hand; but it shall not come nigh thee" (Psa.
91: 7).

The Lord our God goes *before* us as our Leader. He is our
Forerunner and Pioneer in the battle. He is the One Who has
enrolled us as His soldiers (II Tim. 2: 4). "The breaker is gone
up before them: they have broken forth and passed on to the
gate. . . . Their king is passed on before them, and Jehovah at
the head of them" (Micah 2: 13, *cf*. Ex. 13: 21).

The Lord our God protects us from *behind* as our rearguard.
"And the angel of God who went before the camp of Israel,
removed and went behind them; and the pillar of cloud removed
from before them, and stood behind them: and it came between
the camp of Egypt and the camp of Israel . . . and the one came
not near the other" (Ex. 14: 19–20). And finally:

The Lord our God dwells *in* us as the power from on high.
"If a man love me he will keep My words: and My Father will
love him and We will come unto him, and make our abode with
him" (John 14: 23). "Christ in you, the hope of glory" (Col. 1:
27).

So Christ is the Lord on every side of our life. He is above
us and underneath us. He is before us and behind us. He is at
our side and in us. He is "all, and in all" (Col. 3: 11), the
foundation and the goal, the author and perfecter. For this
reason we may have at all times a perfect certainty of victory:
"As the mountains are round about Jerusalem, so the Lord is
round about his people from this time forth and for evermore"
(Psa. 125: 2). Thus, even though sin may beset and surround us
on every side, it has found in Christ, the great Immanuel "God
with us," Who reveals Himself from all sides, its Match and
Master.

In the book of the Prophet Zechariah we read of a remarkable
night vision of the prophet. Four horns appeared. Then
four smiths followed, each obviously armed with a heavy hammer.

F

These four smiths smash with their four hammers the four horns to pieces (Zech. 1: 18–21).

The interpreting angel shows the prophet the meaning of this vision: The four horns represent the hostile world-powers which attack the people of God from every direction. The horn is a symbol of strength. The four smiths are the powers of God which the Lord uses to save His tried elect.

Let us note: It is not a case of three powers of God against four of the enemy but four against four. No power of the enemy is forgotten and no adversary is omitted. *All* of them are to be destroyed. The triumph must be a total one.

Further: it is not the case that four scribes or tailors or businessmen arrive on the scene but four workmen (smiths). This means: God's measures against the enemy are not without strength. They are most powerful. He is not merely equal to His adversaries but far superior. For this reason the city of God can be glad (Psa. 46: 4). For she will win a complete victory finally. The four enemy horns will be totally broken and God's people saved.

And all this by *God's* power. *He* won the victory. "The right hand of the Lord doeth valiantly" (Psa. 118: 15, 16).

Remember: You are *without* power; the enemy is a *strong* power, but God has *all* power. Therefore come with your utter lack of power to Him Who as the Almighty has eternal abundance of power, and you will be able to conquer the enemy's strong power. God's omnipotence is able to make your impotence triumph over all the energy of the adversary.

"*Burdens*" are not the same as "sins." But even burdens hinder us in the race and must therefore be laid aside.

Cares are burdens; for they exhaust spiritual strength. They are an unnecessary load foolishly taken up by ourselves, and they make real running in the race impossible. Certain claims or pretensions are burdens and cripple our activity for Christ. False claims on money hinder missionary sacrifice and practical love and charity. False claims on time encourage selfishness and indolence, make us lazy in going to church, especially to prayer-meetings, in visiting the sick, or in exercising other activities of love. False claims on honour weaken our witness and make us cowardly. They hinder us in the happy confession of our faith and in the willingness to take upon us the shame of Christ.

Without doubt earthly things are a necessity. Time, money, as well as civil and personal honour, are certainly of value for our human existence and are in no wise to be denied on principle. But true spiritual-mindedness will be able to draw the line in each case and to decide what is good and allowable and what can be a "burden" when over-emphasized. The decisive factor is that our inward life should be "apprehended" (laid hold of) by Christ (Phil. 3: 12), so that our heart is an "occupied area." Then we receive a delicate sense for all these differences, so that we remain free as well as bound, realistic with regard to this world as well as ready for sacrificial action for God's Kingdom, natural and spiritual at the same time. Then earthly things will receive their share and heavenly things their fuller portion. Everything depends on temporal things being seen from the standpoint of eternity.

This brings us to the fourth aspect of the right vision of a runner in the race.

4. *Looking to the Goal.* Only if the runner keeps his gaze fixed and concentrated on the goal has he any prospect of victory. For this reason Paul says (and the Hebrews letter moves in just the same lines of thought as the apostle Paul): "Forgetting the things which are behind, and stretching forward to the things which are before, I press on toward the goal unto the prize of the high calling of God in Christ Jesus" (Phil. 3: 13, 14).

Men are not only formed in character by their past (family descent, education) and present circumstances (environment, work and profession), but also very markedly by their future. Man inwardly grows the higher his ideals are. So also in spiritual life hope and sanctification belong together. "And every man that hath this hope set on Him purifieth himself, even as He is pure" (I John 3: 3).

Thus Christ suffered on Golgotha with His eye kept on "the joy that lay before Him" (Heb. 12: 2). As He entered the sombre valley of death His gaze penetrated the darkness around Him and saw already the light of the coming triumph.

This attitude of heart must be ours too. When you suffer shame for the sake of your testimony, rejoice over the future crown of glory. "Every one therefore who shall confess Me before men, him will I also confess before My Father who is in heaven" (Matt. 10: 32). If you renounce the enjoyments of the pleasures of sin for the sake of sanctification and holiness, you may be sure that one day you will be privileged to enjoy

the hidden heavenly manna (Rev. 2: 17).   If you sacrifice money
or goods for the sake of the spread of the gospel be assured that
God is no man's debtor.   Everything which we take out of our
earthly account for His sake is paid into our heavenly account.
"Not that I seek for the gift; but I seek for the fruit that increased
to *your* account" (Phil. 4: 17).   All such expense is in reality
income.

This striving towards the goal thus comprises every outward
and inward realm of life.   The prize is indeed such as to make
it well worth while to give ourselves up wholly to attain it.

In the opening words of Hebrews 12 the writer uses in the
original Greek three remarkable words: "Therefore ... we also!"
(Gk. *toigaroun kai hēmeis*).   The first of them is especially impressive (*toigaroun*).   In other places the New Testament writers,
expressing a very similar thought, use a shorter word for "Therefore" (Gk. only *ara* or *oun* or *dio*).   But in our context a strikingly
emphatic intensification is added to this word (Gk. *toigar* which
serves to emphasize *oun*).   The idea is to emphasize as heavily as
possible the necessity that we New Testament believers shall
draw the practical consequences of the example of the Old
Testament heroes of faith, and especially of the example of Jesus
Christ our Lord.   As if the idea of the word "therefore" were
expressed by three parallel terms following immediately one upon
the other: "Therefore, on this account, for this reason, we also!"

Since the Old Testament saints dedicated themselves fully to
the faith, *Therefore . . . we also!*   Since victory was possible in
previous history at all times, even in times of suffering and trial,
Therefore . . . we also!   Since in the long gallery of faith our forefathers showed heroic courage and endurance in keeping their
eye on the goal, *Therefore . . . we also!*

And above all: Since Christ our Saviour proved it possible to
be victor amidst the sufferings of the cross, and hoped and endured and sacrificed Himself to the end, *Therefore . . . we also!*

And now we must change the plural into the singular, the
"we" must become a "thou."   Because others have been
enabled, Therefore *thou* also.   Since Christ is thy example,
Therefore thou also!   And finally we must get quite personal
and change over from "thou" to "I."   Since Christ has prepared
the way for me, Therefore . . . I also!

In the arena of faith: "*Let us look unto Jesus!*"

CHAPTER V

THE CHRISTIAN RACE AS AN OBSTACLE RACE

THE CHRISTIAN AND SUFFERING

"Ye have not yet resisted unto blood, striving against sin: And ye have forgotten the exhortation which reasoneth with you as with sons, My son, regard not lightly the chastening of the Lord, nor faint when thou art reproved of him: For whom the Lord loveth he chasteneth, and scourgeth every son whom he receiveth. It is for chastening that ye endure; God dealeth with you as with sons; for what son is there whom his father chasteneth not? But if ye are without chastening, whereof all have been made partakers, then are ye bastards, and not sons. Furthermore, we had the fathers of our flesh to chasten us, and we gave them reverence: shall we not much rather be in subjection unto the Father of spirits, and live? For they verily for a few days chastened us as seemed good to them; but he for our profit, that we may be partakers of his holiness. All chastening seemeth for the present to be not joyous but grievous: yet afterward it yieldeth peaceable fruit unto them that have been exercised thereby, even the fruit of righteousness" (Heb. 12: 4–11).

PERSEVERE! Keep running! Hold out to the end! Do not give up or be disheartened! Never look back, but press on towards the mark! With the same freshness as you began at the starting-point, remain steadfast until the goal. Only thus is it possible to gain the prize in the arena, only thus to be crowned. This is the message of the whole Hebrews letter, especially of Hebrews 12.

God is the heavenly Umpire of the race. In His infinite wisdom He has placed obstacles in our way, not indeed to hinder our course, but to test our devotion, to keep us earnest, watchful and persevering, to strengthen our spiritual energy.

Thus the runner's race in the arena of faith is an "obstacle race." There are difficulties and sufferings. Hindrances block our way.   But everything is overruled by the perfect love, wisdom and power of the Divine Umpire.   And the harder the conflict, the more glorious the prize for the victor!

Suffering must be regarded from the view-point of eternity. Only thus can one recognize its high value.   Suffering is not something superfluous or even something that disturbs or restricts our real life and eternal profit.   "My son, *despise not* thou the chastening of the Lord" (v. 5).   We must pay due regard to all the dark mysteries and perplexities of life, for in all of them, in the last analysis, we find—GOD!

He who does not view suffering from God's standpoint, feels himself hindered by difficulties and extremities.   By him suffering will be regarded as mere ballast to keep him steady in the race, and indeed it will actually work itself out as such in his life. Therefore it is essential for the runner in the "arena" to have the right vision of the God-intended meaning of his sufferings, even if he does not understand all His purposes in detail.   Only then can the sufferings be changed into a help instead of a hindrance, into an encouragement instead of a discouragement.   The difficulties of life will support him in his struggle forwards.   That which otherwise appears to paralyse gives him new power. That which seemingly holds him back will really help him to hasten forward.   That which presses him down helps him in fact to look up.   "Let us look up unto Jesus."

Hebrews 12, in the verses just following the opening exhortation to run in the race, shows us in only a few sentences, but in mighty fulness, the blessing of suffering (vv. 5-11).   This is done in a sevenfold manner.

In the obstacle-race of faith the true believer:

sees in the difficulties of this life proofs of the *Fatherhood* of God: (Heb. 12: 5a, 6b, 7b, 8);

regards distresses and trials as ways of the *love* of God: (Heb. 12: 6a);

trusts in the midst of all suffering in the infallibility and fruitfulness of all the decisions of the *wisdom* of God: (Heb. 12: 10a);

reckons, in the whirl of events, with the ordering hand of the all overruling *government* of God: (Heb. 12: 7a);

subjects himself without criticism, even in inexplicable darknesses, to the sovereign *authority* of God: (Heb. 12: 9);

values suffering as a necessity of education, so that our lives are being changed into the image of the *holiness* of God: (Heb. 12: 10);

estimates the darknesses of life as God's means of reaching the bright eternal *goal* of God: (Heb. 12: 11b).

1. *True faith sees in the difficulties of this life* PROOFS OF THE FATHERHOOD OF GOD. Sufferings bear witness to our sonship. 'God dealeth with you as with sons; for what son is there whom his father chasteneth not?" (v. 7). Where discipline is lacking, true fatherhood is wanting. If our earthly fathers, who gave us our bodily life, had to discipline us, how much more God, the Father of spirits, who gave us our intellectual and, above all, our spiritual life?

Therefore it would be wrong and pointless if we should complain by asking: Why does God allow us, His own children, to suffer so much? On the contrary, just *because* we are His sons, God cleanses and educates us. Not in *spite* of His fatherhood but *because* of His fatherhood is His discipline necessary. Thus the sufferings of His children are no ground for disappointment but rather for certainty and thankfulness that He, the eternal God, in Jesus Christ His Son, has become our father. Sufferings are indeed the very proofs of our nobility and standing as belonging to God's family. God speaks to us "as unto children" (v. 5a): He treats us "as sons" (v. 7): He scourges every "son" (v. 6). "Otherwise ye are bastards and not sons" (v. 8). The word here used in the original language for "to scourge" is related etymologically to the Greek word for "child" (Gk. *paideuein*, derived from *pais*, child, boy, girl: Matt. 2: 16; John 4: 51; Luke 8: 51, 54). It means "to bring up someone as a *child*" and, when necessary, "to punish" as a child.

And, with all this, keep in mind that you are not the only son who is being led through dark valleys. God scourges "every" son (v. 6). Thus nothing very extraordinary is happening to you. This, too, may help you not to over-estimate your sufferings. "Knowing that the same afflictions are accomplished in your brethren who are in the world" (I Pet. 5: 9). This makes us careful and reserved in weighing our own burdens, and it can at the same time encourage us, for if the others have been able by the power of the Lord to endure in difficulties and sufferings, then *I* can do likewise. I am not alone, but find myself marching in the midst of a multitude of brothers and sisters who are treading the same path and running in the same obstacle race as myself. Their heavenly Father is also my heavenly Father and He will bring us all to the goal.

2. *True faith regards the distresses and sufferings of this life as*
WAYS OF THE LOVE OF GOD. "For whom the Lord *loveth*, He
chasteneth, and scourgeth every son whom He receiveth" (v. 6).
Sufferings prove that God is interested in us, that He is moulding
us, that He loves us. "Yea, He loveth the peoples; all His saints
are in Thy hand: and they sat down at Thy feet; every one shall
receive of Thy words" (Deut. 33: 3).

What a most astonishing fact! the Almighty God is interested
in our infinitesimally small life! This should suffice us! All
the love of our heavenly Father concerns itself with advancing
our sanctification and blessing us on our way through time to
the land of eternity.

> God's *heart* "loves" us—
>   We are His elect.
> God's *hand* "holds" us—
>   We are under His protection.
> God's *mouth* "teaches" us—
>   We possess His living Word.
> At God's *feet* we are resting—
>   We enjoy His peace.

Thus every child of the heavenly Father can be confident even
in suffering. He knows that "nothing can separate me from the
love of God" (Rom. 8: 38, 39). Yea, even more: All things, and
especially the difficulties, are a *proof* of His love.

Therefore the runner in the race is not discouraged by obstacles. He trusts the love of God and presses on to the goal,
unburdened by cares and sorrows.

Cares are therefore a contradiction of our standing as children
of God. In the Sermon on the Mount, the Lord Jesus warns so
emphatically against all fear and anxiety, that one might rightly
call this part of His discourse a real campaign against the spirit
of worry. The Christian should avoid worry for seven reasons:

(1) Cares and worries are *useless*. With all your worrying you
are not able to add a single cubit to the length of your earthly
pilgrimage. Our earthly pilgrimage is, so to speak, many
thousands of miles in length but we cannot even add as much as
a yard to it (Matt. 6: 27). The translation "stature" is not clear
because it could lead to the idea that the size of the body is meant.
But the Lord wants to point out here that we cannot do even
the smallest things. If, however, we could add a cubit to our

stature that would be an astonishing and remarkably great thing. It would also not at all be desirable, so that nobody would wish or take much care and thought to be able to do it! For this reason the text in question can be understood only in the sense that the length of our earthly pilgrimage is meant. A cubit here would indeed be something very small. We cannot lengthen our life even for a few minutes however much thought or worrying we might take.

(2) Cares and worries are *injurious*. They are unnecessary and foolish hindrances. For if one worries one experiences each difficulty twice: the first time in one's imagination and the second time in reality, the first time in expectancy, the second time in the actual event. But once would suffice! "Sufficient unto the day is the evil thereof" (Matt. 6: 34). Therefore: "Never worry worry till worry worries you. Never trouble trouble till trouble troubles you."

(3) Cares and worries are *unworthy*. The lilies of the field and the fowls of the air do not worry and yet are looked after. Art thou not better than they? The pictures used by the Lord are very apt.

Food and raiment are the main objects of worry. The fowls refer to food and are a picture from the animal world; the lilies refer to raiment and are a picture from the plant world. Sowing and reaping is men's work, while sewing and spinning is especially women's work. All these points of view are summarized as follows:

the question of food and raiment,
the picture from the animal world and the plant world;
sowing and reaping and sewing and spinning,
the sphere of men's and that of women's work—

all this unites in the impressive harmonious demand: "Be not anxious for your life" (Matt. 6: 25). Worrying is a denial of the nobility of man. For man is better than a flower or an animal. He is the crown of creation and destined for a kingdom.

All worrying is undignified. He who worries is forgetting his high calling, as well as the willingness and power of our great God to help. He is forgetting God's all-sufficiency and perfect wisdom as well as His eternal love.

(4) Cares and worries are *unfilial*. It being already true from the view-point of creation, that man as man is much higher than the plants and animals, how much more must it be true from the

view-point of salvation! As children of our heavenly Father we can happily and thankfully trust that: "Your heavenly Father knoweth that ye have need of all these things" (Matt. 6: 32). The spirit of worrying in a child of God means, therefore, that he is leaving his heavenly rank out of account. It belongs to the privileges and obligations of a practical realization of our standing as sons of God that we happily trust our Father.

(5) Cares and worries are *earthly*. They direct our questionings and thoughts far too much to things here below (food and raiment); but the attitude of mind of the believer should have a heavenly direction: "But seek ye first the kingdom of God and His righteousness; and all these things shall be added unto you" (Matt. 6: 33).

(6) Cares and worries are *idolatrous*. They concern themselves too much with the question of having or not having earthly things. And that is a service of Mammon. In the Sermon on the Mount the Greek text leaves out the definite article "the" before the word "mammon," thus purposely treating this word as a personal name. "Mammon" is, so to speak the name of a god as Apollo or Diana are names of heathen deities. "No man can serve two masters (two gods): God Jehovah and false god Mammon" (Matt. 6: 24).

(7) Cares and worries are *heathenish*. "For after all these things do the Gentiles seek" (Matt. 6: 32). The spirit of worrying represents an attitude of mind which is foreign to the kingdom of God. It lowers the thinking of the redeemed to the standard of that of the unredeemed, so that though he lives in the kingdom of grace, he behaves himself as one who is outside, like a heathen.

For all these reasons cares and worries must be avoided by the Christian. "Cast all your anxiety upon Him; for He careth for you" (I Pet. 5: 7).

In his pithy manner of expression Luther once said: "Oh, that we could learn this sort of 'casting'! But he who does not learn it will remain a man downcast, outcast, cast off, cast behind, cast away."

On the other hand living faith will recognize the truth of that other saying of the great Reformer:

> To count out money from an empty purse,
> To bake bread from the clouds,
> This is the art of our God alone.
> He makes all things out of nothing
> And He doeth it daily.

Two passages of Scripture express strikingly opposite aspects of truth. Both refer emphatically to the question of providing for the outward life. The second is given in the chapter immediately subsequent to Hebrews 12 and thus is in a certain, indirect connexion with our chapter (Heb. 13: 5). The first is the most positive and the other the most negative sentence of the whole New Testament. In a very small space the first passage contains five affirmations and the second five negations. Here is the first passage:

"God is able to make *all* grace abound toward you; that ye, *al*ways having *all* sufficiency in *all* things, may abound unto every (lit. *all*) good work" (II Cor. 9: 8). In the Greek the root word for "all" occurs five times in this one passage (*pasan, panti, pantote, pasan, pan*).

The other Scripture reads: "I will in no wise fail thee, neither will I in any wise forsake thee" (Heb. 13: 5).

In both cases it is hardly possible to give the literal order of the Greek words in the original text, especially in the second passage. The first part of this sentence contains a double and the second part a triple negative, so that the sentence contains a fivefold negation, as if the text should read: " *Not* will I fail thee! *Nevermore! No! Never* and by *no* means will I forsake thee!"

Thus these two Scriptures show in their harmonious contrast, positively and negatively expressed, the same precious message:

Will God give me all things which are necessary and good?— Yes! Five times yes!—"All grace! In all things! Always! All sufficiency! All good work!"

Will God ever forsake me?—No! Five times no!—"Never! Nevermore! Never and by no means! In no circumstances!"

Therefore: "Have faith in God!" His love and His faithfulness rule over our life.

The obstacles in the race are appointed and overruled by His perfect Divine wisdom. All arrangements in the racecourse are made by Himself Who is both our wise and just Umpire and our loving heavenly Father.

3. *True faith trusts in the midst of all suffering in the infallibility and fruitfulness of all the* DECISIONS OF THE WISDOM OF GOD. Earthly fathers, even though they may be very experienced, and full of love and wisdom in the selection of their methods of upbringing, can, nevertheless, make mistakes. They must always

act only within a certain more or less restricted horizon of their outlook and are always liable to error common to man. The best and highest they can do is to take all their decisions according to their best knowledge and conscience. But the heavenly Father never makes mistakes. His discipline never errs. In His loving treatment of His children He never takes a wrong measure. Everything is chosen to serve His ends. Everything is planned to reach the great, ideal goal, and this goal is indeed the highest possible, namely to transform His child into the image of His own holy nature. "For they verily for a few days chastened us as seemed good [or meet] to them; but He for our profit that we may become partakers of His holiness" (Heb. 12: 10). Thus faith can rest not only in God's love but also in His wisdom. Faith knows, "I am God's child and not His counsellor" (Tersteegen). Even when I am in the midst of tribulation and trial and see no way out, I can say: His hand holds me fast. My Father rules over everything and He knows!

> Be still, my soul: The Lord is on thy side;
>   Bear patiently the cross of grief or pain;
> Leave to thy God to order and provide;
>   In every change He faithful will remain.
> Be still, my soul; thy best thy heavenly Friend
> Through thorny ways leads to a joyful end.
>
> Be still, my soul: thy God doth undertake
>   To guide the future as He has the past.
> Thy hope, thy confidence let nothing shake;
>   All now mysterious shall be bright at last.
> Be still, my soul: the waves and winds still know
> His voice who ruled them while He dwelt below.
>
>   *Katharina von Schlegel*
>   (*Tr. Jane L. Borthwick*).

The whole situation is however completed, and becomes a matter of actual comfort and help for troubled redeemed ones, when they remember that it is not only the perfect love and wisdom of the Father which rules here but also His Divine omnipotence. Our heavenly Father *wants* to help, *knows how* to help and *is able* to help. This trinity of Divine powers gives us, in their working together, the guarantee that, in spite of the difficulties and hardships on the way, at the end everything will come out for our good. In fact, looking at the matter from

God's point of view, we can say that, because everything is under His overruling hand, everything is profitable and good even today.

4. *True faith reckons in the whirl of events with the ordering hand of the* ALL OVERRULING GOVERNMENT OF GOD. The leading thought of our passage in Hebrews 12 is, no doubt, that the sufferings of the redeemed have a deeper meaning than their outward appearance (Heb. 12: 11), that with all the activities of the enemies, *God* in reality is the acting One, that although the persecutors of the Christians aim at their destruction, the real God-intended aim in all these events is their glorification, their "profit," the "peaceable fruit of righteousness." "What ye endure is for your upbringing" (v. 7a): "*God* dealeth with you . . . for your profit" (vv. 7 and 10). For "afterward" suffering, even the suffering of persecution of which the verses under consideration chiefly speak, will give to those who are exercised thereby a peaceable fruit of righteousness (v. 11). This means that God overrules even the actions of His enemies. They thought evil against us but God meant it unto good (Gen. 50: 20). God uses the aims of the godless to reach and attain His own Divine aims. He acts in a mysterious veiling of Himself in such a manner that even faith can recognize it only to a limited degree. In all the manifold single events He never loses His outlook over the whole. He is not only the God of all collectively, but also the God of each individual. In all the great events He never forgets the small matters, in the universal history never the personal life-story, in the course of centuries never the happenings of seconds. He holds all the reins of events in His hand, in all the complicated network of happenings of time and space, of men and history.

Faith can therefore take the actions of unbelievers as being sent to him from God. They would not have been able to place the disturbances and obstacles in our racecourse if they had not been allowed to do so by the heavenly Organizer of the contest, and if the mighty Divine Umpire, in a mysterious, yet most effective way, were not acting Himself behind and in all their endeavours.

This gives us a remarkable sense of independence of man and of superiority in all the changing scenes of life. "So now it was *not you* that sent me hither, but *God*" (Gen. 45: 8) were the words of Joseph to his brethren, although he knew perfectly well what had happened and although he had just presented himself to them with the words: "I am Joseph, your brother, whom *ye* sold into Egypt" (v. 4). Three times he stated: "*God* did send me before you" (v. 5), "*God* sent me before you" (v. 7), "*God* meant it unto good to bring to pass, as it is this day, to save much people alive" (Gen. 50: 20). Thus faith, in the last analysis, accepts nothing from the hands of men; faith accepts all things from the hands of a great, loving, almighty, ruling God, including all the difficulties and losses, even the injustices which he has to suffer. "Shall there be evil in a city, and the Lord has not done it?" (Amos 3: 6). Here we encounter a mighty secret of God's world-government, the power of which we have to recognize obediently and trustfully, although we cannot understand with our human intellect the various detail connexions and relationships of His plan. It makes us extremely happy thus to know that: "Everything which reaches us in life must first have passed before God."

For this reason the Scriptures never speak of a mere "permissive" will of God. God is never a mere spectator. His attitude is not passive in the happenings of this world, but definitely active. He is not *beside* the events, but *in* them. He is not only the One Who lives *above* the world, He lives also *in* the world: "for *in* Him we live and move and have our being" (Acts 17: 28). This was not stated by the apostle in a purely spiritual sense, as though thereby he meant exclusively believers; no, he is speaking here of men in general as the creatures of God, in fact even of heathen also.

God's eternal plan for the Kingdom governs our life. All the happenings of human history are scaffolding for the happenings of the history of salvation. Heaven and hell, angels and demons, faith and infidelity, church and world, great and small, the general and the personal things of this life, everything must serve, consciously or unconsciously, willingly or unwillingly, to fulfil the will of *God*. He ruleth and doeth all things well.

For this reason we know that "to them that love God, all things work together for good, to them who are the called according to His purpose" (Rom. 8: 28). In this verse is expressed the servitude of all earthly relationships to the will of God. Everything "worketh together" (literally). All earthly things serve heavenly ends. By means of all things, even by means of "the worst things," the "best" shall be reached, *i.e.*, the transformation of the redeemed into the image of Christ the Redeemer, so that they may become "conformed to the image of

His Son, that He might be the Firstborn among many brethren"
(Rom. 8: 29).

It is expressly declared, however, that this happens only in
the case of "those who love God."   For "earthly things must be
known before we can love them; but Divine things must be loved
before we can get to know them" (Pascal).   And not in vain are
these who love God characterized at the same time as those "who
are the called according to His purpose."   This means to say:
An eternal plan governs our life.   Our short life on earth lies
between two eternities: the eternity before the time of the world,
with its Divine election, and the eternity after this world, with
its glorious perfection.   All the circumstances of time have been
considered and allowed for in God's eternal planning.   If
therefore all the happenings and relationships of time here below
serve together to work out the final realization of the Divine
plan, this means that no circumstances which appear from time
to time are unprepared for, or mere coincidences, or even matters
of chance in each existing situation, but are rather evidences of
the eternal forethought in the counsel of our gracious God.
Thus our assurance of faith that everything temporal is but a link
in the chain of the eternal, is founded on a firm rock.   And con-
fidently reckoning with the omnipotent government of a loving
God and Father we can pass along even dark and dangerous roads
in life without anxiety or fear.

5.   *True faith even in inexplicable darknesses subjects itself without
criticism to the* SOVEREIGN ROYAL AUTHORITY OF GOD.   This is
also emphasized in our passage in Hebrews: "Furthermore we
had fathers of our flesh to chasten us, and we gave them reverence: shall we not much rather be in subjection unto the Father
of spirits, and live?" (Heb. 12: 9).   This means: it is a condition
of real life to be subject to the Father of spirits.   To subject
oneself and to live are two things which belong inseparably
together.   Should we not be able to bow to the disciplinary and
educational measures of our heavenly Father without contra-
dicting, without inward rebellion, and with thankful, quiet and
happy hearts?   Are not His thoughts infinitely higher than our
thoughts? (Isa. 55: 8–9).   Is He not able to judge the situation
better than we, He living in the High and Holy Place, on His
eternal throne in the heavenly heights?   But we live in the
plains here below, in the narrow and deep valleys of this earthly
life and therefore we can have but a restricted and very small
horizon.   May it not be that many things which here appear

to us to be utterly senseless and meaningless will be revealed to
us in eternity as being most meaning*ful* and of the greatest
importance?

Does He, the Divine Organizer of the race, not know better
what arrangements are necessary and profitable for the runner
than the runner himself, who is always only one individual par-
ticipant in the contest, but can never have the complete survey of
the whole?   Is therefore the racer not under the obligation simply
to acknowledge the superiority and authority of the Divine
Umpire and, without any arguing, to undertake the running with
all its arrangements and obstacles, just as this race by the heavenly
Organizer has been "set before him"?

But if we complain and worry and distrust our heavenly Father,
it means that we regard Him less and give Him less reverence
than we did our earthly fathers.   For our earthly fathers we did
trust, even if they sometimes corrected us.   And is it right to
rebel against our heavenly Father if He takes us into His school
of discipline and leads us through difficulties and trials only in
order to further our spiritual life, and, indeed, to show us in
the very experience of suffering His loving-kindness and
care?

Moreover He is far superior to all earthly fathers.   They were
our fathers after the flesh; but He is the Father of spirits.   Therefore He, our heavenly Father, is as much superior to our
earthly fathers as the spirit is more than the body and as the
inward spiritual personality is more than the external bodily
appearance.

Therefore away with all grumbling!   All spirit of complaint
and dissatisfaction is rebellion against God.   God is always
right.   "Love your destiny, for it is God's way with your soul."
Even if a thousand enigmas surround you, even if you can see no
way out and everything appears senseless, *faith can wait*.   God's
books must be read backwards, that is, from the end to the
beginning.   But having once reached the goal, looking back, we
shall see that all darknesses of our path will have become radiantly
bright.

Until eternity dawns God dwelleth in darkness.   The nearer
the priest came to the centre of the symbolical dwelling-place of
Jehovah in the tabernacle and approached the throne of grace,
that is, the ark of the covenant with the mercy-seat, and the
shekinah, the darker it became round about him.   The Outer
Court was without roof and illuminated by the natural light of the

sun: the Holy Place was lighted by the subdued light of the lamp-stand in the totally enclosed room. The Most Holy Place was, however, absolutely dark. "The Lord said that He would dwell in the thick darkness" (I Kings 8: 12; *cf.* Ex. 20: 21). The meaning of this is as follows: The nearer a man comes to God, the more he approaches The Great Mystery. God is the Eternal One, the Absolutely Different One, the great Superior One. Absolute infinity is of His essence. No human intelligence can fathom the depths of His Divine being. Before Him we can only acknowledge our own smallness and humble and bow our-selves. In His presence we can only recognize and wonder at His Majesty, keep silence, and worship.

God "dwelleth in the light unapproachable" (I Tim. 6: 16). His earthly symbolic dwelling-place was meant to bear witness to this fact. In the symbolic language, however, of tabernacle and temple His invisibility could be represented only by the lack of all created light. The absolute eternal light could only be expressed by mystical symbolical darkness.

In the eternal city of God His face will be seen (Rev. 22: 4; Matt. 5: 8). Therefore when that time has come the heavenly Holiest of Holies will be no more dark, without illumination, but filled with streams of light (Rev. 21: 10, 11, 23). "For the Lord God giveth them light" (Rev. 22: 5). "For we shall see Him even as He is" (I John 3: 2). "Then shall I know even as also I have been known." This will be a marvellous experience both in respect to God's general counsel of salvation and with regard to His personal, often so mysterious, ways by which He has led the individual.

One thing especially will be revealed: God's dealings with us in suffering were always designed to be a help to our spiritual growth.

6. *True faith values suffering as a necessity of education, so that our lives should be changed into the* IMAGE OF THE HOLINESS OF GOD. The heavenly Father chasteneth us for "our profit" in order that we might be "partakers of His holiness" (Heb. 12: 10). "Needs are often needful because many things prosper only in times of need." God's measures to help must sometimes be onerous or even severe. For it is true that "Small trials often make us *beside* ourselves, but great trials bring us again back *to* ourselves." It was when the prodigal son "came to himself" that he said, "I will arise and go to my father," and this was caused by hunger (Luke 15, 14–18).

In all times of "visitation" God is endeavouring to "visit" us. He is seeking us and is striving to persuade us, the fugitives from God, to return home, to come back to the Father's house. In this sense even the disappointments in life are intended to awaken us out of all illusions into which sin has led us, for instance, as if we ourselves were so important and as if in our life earthly things were the true values that really matter.

The sufferings of this world are a means in the hands of God for the realization of His plan for man's redemption. Precisely the fact that the earth cannot give what man seeks and desires, delivers him from his false expectations and stirs up his yearnings for Paradise lost. The disappointments in the earthly thus help to make man free to long for the heavenly, so that at the end of the way he can confess: "Behold, it was for my peace that I had great bitterness" (Isa. 38: 17).

Thus the obstacles in our race are intended by God's purposeful love to further our inner development, to strengthen our spiritual muscles, to give us opportunities for victory, to help us to be more and more transformed, in character and conduct, into practical accordance with the holy nature of the eternal goal. Finally:

7. *True faith estimates the darknesses of life as God's means of reaching the* BRIGHT, ETERNAL GOAL OF GOD. "Pressure raises up!" The "afterward" will soon be the present. "All chastening seemeth for the present to be not joyous, but grievous: yet afterward it yieldeth peaceable fruit unto them that have been exercised thereby, even the fruit of righteousness" (Heb. 12: 11).

To be sure, even the Christian feels the sharpness of difficulties. They are real to him also. They "appear" to be troublesome, and the Bible does not blame us for feeling so. The things of God are always far too natural than to make unnatural demands on human faculties and possibilities. The Bible never goes so far as to require of the Christian to disregard his trials and to look upon them superficially, as though difficulties were no difficulties and distresses no distresses. If the Christian were expected to do this, trials would have no meaning for him and would in fact be no longer "trials" and consequently without any fruit and effect. No, if God's strokes brought us no pain, they would no longer be a help for us to overcome our sins. But just because they hurt, they help us. The Scripture uses even the very strong word "scourgeth" (Heb. 12: 6). The Greek word used here, *mastigoi*, is related to the word for "whip" (Gk. *mastix*). Compare Acts 22: 24; Heb. 11: 36.

Of Job we read that before he uttered those wondrous words, "The Lord gave, and the Lord hath taken away; blessed be the name of the Lord" (Job 1: 21), he had felt and expressed his deepest sorrow and pain after having received the news of the catastrophes. Indeed he had shown his mourning and grief quite openly: "Then Job arose, and rent his mantle, and shaved his head, and fell down upon the ground" (v. 20). It may be that this sense of the sharpness of the sufferings may even dim for a time the spiritual vision of our heart. And we know that the heavenly High Priest has understanding for even this, for He is touched with the feeling of our infirmities (Heb. 4: 15). The agonies of trial sometimes may blur our inward sight. But he who keeps on trusting will experience finally that the ways of God with His own are never to be compared with one having to go into a dark cave, or into some subterranean labyrinth with endless, unlit, black passages which, so to speak, swallow us up and hold us captive without any way out for ever; the ways of God are rather to be compared to passing through a narrow, and often indeed long, tunnel, which at first leads downwards into darkness and depth, but at the other end, "afterward," leads up into sunshine, all the more glorious and brilliant.

This "afterward" is often experienced in anticipation while we are yet on the way. Sufferings are seeds to bring forth the fruit of peace and righteousness. He who is exercised and practised in hardships will harvest the "fruit" of this seed-sowing. Great peace enters his heart; true righteousness fills his standing and his state. Thus he acquires a "fruit" which as to the state of his heart is called "peaceable," and with respect to his standing and practical state in life is called "righteousness."

Every time we stand the test, we further our spiritual progress. God's angels minister to us after every victory (*cf.* Matt. 4: 11). Growth in sanctification increases our joy.

The peaceable fruit of righteousness grows on the apparently crooked and wild tree of tribulation. This heavenly fruit as to its character is "righteousness" and as to its taste "peace." God works in us a practical righteousness of life and walk which is based upon the righteousness of our standing which we have received through faith in Christ Jesus (Phil. 3: 9).

Righteousness produces peace, holiness, purity, and joy. The character of the new life is righteousness, its inward harmony and enjoyment peace.

Perhaps the expression "peace" as the fruit of righteousness looks back to the first verses of Hebrews 12, where the arena of faith is mentioned. At the end of the race, when the battle is won, we shall enjoy the fruit of righteousness in peace.

> Light after darkness,
>   Gain after loss,
> Strength after weakness,
>   Crown after cross,
> Sweet after bitter,
>   Hope after fears,
> Home after wandering,
>   Praise after tears.
>
> Sheaves after sowing,
>   Sun after rain,
> Sight after mystery,
>   Peace after pain,
> Joy after sorrow,
>   Calm after blast,
> Rest after weariness,
>   Sweet rest at last.
>
> (*Frances Ridley Havergal.*)

All the apparent hindrances in life are thus in reality further-ances. Should we not therefore, in the midst of tribulation, be "in subjection unto the Father of spirits, and live"? (Heb. 12: 9). This means to "live" in the deep spiritual sense of the word. "Life," not meaning merely "being" in the sense of just existing, but rather as being filled with strength, joy, real meaning and purpose, yea, a being filled indeed with God and Christ.

"Tribulation does not destroy faith, but confirms it. Tribula-tion is not the messenger of the wrath of God, but rather of His goodness. Tribulation does not exclude us from our fellow-ship with God, but rather prepares us for the full enjoyment of His grace in His presence."

Faith therefore believes against all human reasonings to the contrary. Faith knows that while God sometimes appears to be only the taking One, He is in reality always the giving One. Indeed, just *in* taking and *by* taking He often is giving. But He gives after His own fashion, which is often very different from ours. And then He often fulfils our expectations by apparently disappointing them. His ways are wiser than ours; His thoughts are higher than our thoughts (Isa. 55: 9), and He is always right. For this we shall one day praise Him eternally.

Mary wept by the open grave of the Lord. She saw her loss. Not even the dead body of her Master was there any more. And yet that very empty tomb was the proof of the resurrection, the sign of victory, and, had she rightly understood the situation, it would have given her abundant reason for triumphant joy. But how wonderfully "afterward" her lamentation was turned to jubilation! (Matt. 28: 8). "Mary—Rabboni"—how much is contained in those few words! (John 20: 16). And after she had understood the *real* meaning of the empty tomb, think how this knowledge made her to be a witness to the resurrection, a proclaimer of the mightiest triumph of life, a joyful testifier to the victorious power of the Risen One! (Luke 24: 10).

Thus for the redeemed everything has a twofold aspect: *Nature and faith*. From the natural point of view we often see only the loss; faith, however, sees the gain. From the natural point of view we see death, but faith sees resurrection and life.

Nature sees the tomb, faith the resurrection. Nature looks woefully back into the treasures of memory, faith looks forward to the coming glory. So faith becomes joyful expectancy and hope. It is waiting for the day of redemption and our being clothed upon with the body of glory.

Then the day of the true, real "afterward" will have come. The goal will have been reached for which we strove in the arena of faith. And when the crowns and prizes have been bestowed, the runner in the race will praise the Captain of his faith especially for the difficulties which He, the great Umpire of the race, in His wisdom and love had placed in his path. Truly there had been many obstacles in his way, sometimes even hindrances which seemed to overcome him; but in reality all these hindrances had been like obstacles in an "obstacle race," especially ordained by the organizer of the race. And our heavenly Umpire never makes a mistake. He places the "obstacles" in our way in order to test the spiritual strength and energy of the runner, to exercise him, to strengthen him, and thus to bring him all the more surely and with all the more glory to the winning-post.

Then the day of eternity will dawn, the day which knows no evening or sunset. Its sun will arise, the heavenly light will shine forth, and everything will be radiant and clear in the full and everlasting daylight of God's glory.

Then we shall worship Him who guided us here below. We shall praise Him for all His ways with us, admire His wisdom and enjoy His never-ending love, and the vision of His face will be our everlasting delight.

CHAPTER VI

PRESSING ON TO THE MARK!

"Wherefore lift up the hands that hang down, and the palsied knees; and make straight paths for your feet, that that which is lame be not turned out of the way; but rather be healed. Follow after peace with all men, and the sanctification without which no man shall see the Lord: Looking carefully lest there be any man that falleth short of the grace of God; lest any root of bitterness springing up trouble you, and thereby the many be defiled" (or poisoned) (Heb. 12: 12–15).

CHRISTIANITY is eternity in time. With the appearance o Christ a new sprig was planted into the withered ground of the world of man. And all who have been grafted into it have become partakers of eternal life. Thus Christians have found the fountain of eternal youth. The genuine life of faith never grows old. "Though our outward man is decaying, yet our inward man is renewed day by day" (II Cor. 4: 16). "They that wait upon the Lord shall renew their strength; they shall mount up with wings as eagles; they shall run, and not be weary; they shall walk, and not faint" (Isa. 40: 31). A really healthy life of faith is like one running in an arena whose freshness of the starting-post is maintained to the finish.

And yet! The Christians of the letter to the Hebrews had grown tired. After a richly blessed start (Heb. 10: 32) their inward life had begun to droop. Their hands were hanging down and their knees had become feeble (Heb. 12: 12). The attendance at their gatherings had decreased (Heb. 10: 25). Their life of faith was no longer to be compared to running in an arena but rather to the slow and painful walk of a sick or paralysed person. Instead of looking towards the goal, they began to turn their eyes to times gone by. Instead of looking forward to the consummation at the coming of Christ, they looked backward to the Old Testament ages of preparation. Instead of considering the glories of the Spirit and the fulfilment of all prophecy in Christ's person and work, they began to yearn for the types and symbols of the Divine service of the Old Covenant which they had known as so beautiful and impressive. So the glory of grace had become darkened for them. It appeared desirable to them to return to the law. The danger of "being hardened" had arisen (Heb. 3: 13). Indeed, they had even to be told: "Take heed, brethren, lest there be in any one of you an evil heart of unbelief, in falling away from the living God" (Heb. 3: 12).

How can they be helped?

Only by renewed contact with the Fountain of power. The exceeding glory and reality of the New Testament salvation must come before their minds and hearts as a fresh vision. They must be brought to acknowledge that leaving the ground of grace means robbing oneself, returning to the old is sinking into the depth, turning back to the past is losing the future. Only grace can lead to the goal. Only the New Testament type of salvation can guarantee the promised eternal glory.

For this reason the main purpose of *Hebrews* is, as to its essence, a message of "reformation." No doubt the letter to the Hebrews contains a good deal of doctrine. In fact, it is *the* document of the New Testament which gives us the deepest insight into the inward relationships of preparation and fulfilment, of shadow and reality, of Old Testament sacrifices and the New Testament priesthood of Christ. But the chief object is not that of instruction but of renewal, not that of doctrinal presentation but of practical restoration, not that of leading the readers for the first time *into* the knowledge of full salvation, but rather that of leading them *back* to that which they had already acknowledged and experienced from the very start of their Christian life. Here the reader is not encouraged to lay hold on salvation but rather to hold it fast. It is not so much the matter of being "formed" as of being "re-formed."

For this reason *Hebrews* is, within the New Testament, the sister letter to the Epistle to the Galatians. In both letters the purpose is the same. They are the main "reformatory" epistles of the New Testament.

In the Galatian letter, as also in the *Hebrews*, people are dealt with who were in danger of falling back from the New Testament heights of salvation to the Old Testament introductory stages of Divinely revealed history. The main difference is that the Galatian Christians were originally heathen who had since come under wrong Hebrew-Christian influences, while the leaders of the letters to the Hebrews were Israelites who had accepted the Messiah, perhaps even priests or Levites (Acts 6: 7).

This made a different type of presentation of thought necessary.

"Law and grace" is the theme of both letters. But the Galatian letter treats it with special reference to the *moral* laws of the Mosaic dispensation, while the *Hebrews* speaks especially of its *ceremonial* laws. The Galatian letter refers chiefly to jurisdiction, *Hebrews* to worship and cult (Divine Service).

In *Galatians* Paul points out that it is not allowable in law to alter testamentary documents which have already been officially recognized (Gal. 3: 15–20), and he speaks of legal forms of the educational system of antiquity (Gal. 3: 23–29), and of the respective legal position of slaves and of sons before they become of age (Gal. 4: 1–7). So the Galatian letter uses pictures and comparisons taken more from the *legal* practice, but *Hebrews* (especially chs. 5–10) refers more to the *symbolical* language of the Old Testament forms of Divine Service, to priesthood, sacrifice, tabernacle. *Galatians* places us more in a law-court, *Hebrews* in a temple.

But the theme is the same: the relationship of law to grace, the greater glory of grace, freely bestowed, and, as the result of this, the holy demand and serious warning: *Never go back!* "Hold that fast which thou hast, that no one take thy crown" (Rev. 3: 11).

I. PARALYSING POWERS

How did it come about that the Hebrew Christians lost their original freshness of faith? How happy they had been at the beginning! What would they not have done for Christ in those early days? They received into their houses the persecuted witnesses of Christ (Heb. 10: 34). They endured personally all sorts of indignities and trials (Heb. 10: 33). Even the loss of their possessions on account of their Christian confession they had endured, and had done it not only without complaining, but, indeed, with rejoicing. "Ye took joyfully the spoiling of your goods" (Heb. 10: 34).

And now everything had become different. Instead of the former freshness and vigour, their hands hung down, instead of marching manfully onwards, a paralysis had set in. They no longer pressed on, running on the racecourse, but had halted, and indeed were in danger of stagnation. In fact many had definitely become backsliders (Heb. 12: 12, 13). The enemy had begun his work of inducing paralysis.

1. *The external difficulties* had been used by him in order to weaken and to eliminate these joyful witnesses of God. Again and again they had to meet with bitter hatred against Christ. Continually the world mocked at and despised them. Ever and again outward loss, social ostracism, and injury in their business or professional standing made them feel the lack of legal rights. By all this the enemy had been able to wear them down. It was not the first shock of suffering that brought him this success but the continuing pressure of persecution.

However, the extremity of persecution had not yet been reached. Martyrs' blood had not yet flowed. And this fact is used by the writer of the Hebrews letter to encourage them: "ye have not yet resisted unto blood, striving against sin" (Heb. 12: 4). This is not intended to mean that "You have not yet taken seriously enough the struggle against your own sin which is *within* yourselves. You have not yet shown sufficient energy of faith, readiness for service, devotion, initiative, and resolution in your personal sanctification." But the sin which is spoken of here is the persecuting might of the enemy and the world which approaches from *outside*. It is meant not as the subjective, but as the objective power of evil, of the enmity of the world; so that the meaning is that "the battle has not yet become so fierce that some of you have had to die for the sake of the testimony of Christ." So far there has not been shedding of blood. Though the situation was hard enough, they had thus far been spared the hardest of all.

But they must remember that others had made this supreme sacrifice! The immediately preceding chapter, Hebrews 11, had spoken of those who had been "stoned" or "sawn asunder," who had been tortured, or put to death by the sword, and who had accepted no deliverance, though they could have obtained it easily, if only by one word or one action they had denied their faith (Heb. 11: 35–37). But they refused to do this in order "that they might obtain a better resurrection" than such an earthly deliverance, which last might have been comparable to a "resurrection" by being immediately freed from prison and martyrdom. And now, though certainly recognizing the seriousness of your present situation, how much less are your difficulties! Therefore do not *overestimate* your hardships!

And have we today not much more reason to keep in mind this same exhortation? What are our sufferings for the testimony compared with those of many men and women in the glorious history of the heroes of the church of former times?

In the course of my travels I have often visited places where Christians in times gone by suffered death for their faith. Think of the dreadful subterranean prison cells hewn into the frightful fortress of the Spilberg in *Brünn* (Moravia). Or think of Prague, where 27 crosses, composed of small stones in the pavement in front of the old Town Hall, remind us today of the "Bloody Judgment" of Prague (1620, two years after the beginning of the Thirty Years' War). Small paving-stones mark also the exact spot of the scaffold on which the 27 leaders of the Protestants were beheaded. They are in the form of a large crown of thorns, with two long, crossed judgment swords. Think of the cells of the Bloody Tower on the Thames in London, where one can still see under glass plates verses of the Bible and comforting words which were carved into the walls by those men in the times of their greatest distress. Or I think of the market-place in Florence where the gallows and stake of the great Italian forerunner of the Reformation, Savonarola, stood. I remember walking through the catacombs of ancient Rome, with the secret meeting-places of the early Christians during the times of the persecutions, and in the arena of the Colosseum in Rome where hundreds of witnesses to the faith in the second and third centuries allowed themselves to be torn in pieces by wild animals. Only a few years ago I stood in the evening twilight in the graveyard of the Scottish town of Kilmarnock at the side of the graves of seven whose blood was shed about 300 years ago for their unflinching stand for their Biblical evangelical faith. Just before this we had held an open-air meeting in the market-place of the town at which I had opportunity to give my testimony. The place where we stood with our gospel caravan and loudspeaker was very significant to me. It was just over against the spot where the "Covenanter," John Lisbet, was executed in 1688 (14th of April), a man who had pledged himself not to deny the Biblical "covenant" of faith and who had been willing to suffer the sentence of death. Here again the exact spot where the gallows stood is marked by special small paving-stones. Many of these heroic Scottish Covenanters signed with their own blood their "covenant" never to deny Christ or His word. And now we stood on exactly the same spot and proclaimed exactly the same message for the sake of which this man had laid down his life. Afterwards I went with a Scottish friend to an old, historic cemetery. The stars had already come out and quietly we stood at the gravesides of seven others of these witnesses of Christ. Special framed inscriptions show the site.

How small and feeble one feels, standing on such spots! A feeling of veneration and reverence comes over one for these heroes of God in whom the might of Christ was so powerful! Those were men and women for whom Christ meant more than their own life. And we ourselves are often so timid and do not give a clear testimony. How often we tend to make compromises! How easily we are afraid of being put at a disadvantage, or of not being promoted in life and profession, or of having to hear a sarcastic remark or getting a "superior" look, a shrug of the shoulders, or even only to be smiled or laughed at. But the Lord wants fighters, men who really sacrifice themselves for His interests, men who have counted the cost of true Christianity and who are prepared to pay it. In truth we are in the same position as the Hebrew Christians: we have not yet resisted unto blood. Blood has not yet been demanded from us. Therefore we must not overestimate the difficulties which we take upon ourselves for Christ's sake. On the other hand, come what may, we want to be ready for anything.

The real reason, however, for the signs of fatigue, noticeable amongst the Hebrew Christians, was not so much their externally difficult situation, but their internal reaction to it. Inwardly they had become weak. And therein lay the real root of the danger of their failure.

2. *Inward weakness and signs of fatigue.* Their prayer life had slackened, the numbers at their gatherings had decreased, and their spiritual energy had fallen off. They were to be compared to a pilgrim who had roused himself to leave the "City of Destruction" in order to go to the heavenly Jerusalem but who had become tired and weary on the way and could now only force himself forward with "feeble knees" (Heb. 12: 12).

Their actions and ambitions were no more those of the athlete in a race. They were in danger of giving up the battle altogether. No longer were they runners who were "pressing on." Old attractions of their former worship which had long since been eclipsed, and had lost their glory by Christ having risen as the Sun in their hearts, began to shine again. Their whole life of sanctification had become problematic, and with this also their

attaining the radiant goal and their abundant entry into the high
glories of their heavenly calling.   So that it was necessary to
exhort them: "Follow (lit., pursue) . . . the sanctification without
which no man shall see the Lord" (Heb. 12: 14).   *Run* in the
race (v. 1).

And what shall *we* do?   It is not our task to rebuke these
Hebrew Christians.   Is it not a fact that the picture of their
situation is far too often an exact description of our own inward
state?   What about our own zeal?   How often do we go to
hear God's word and to pray?   Do we regularly take part in the
prayer-meetings of our churches and assemblies, striving together
by prayer in the battle of the Lord?   If we do not, our knees are
"paralysed."   Does peace rule among us?   Do we watch over
our fellow-pilgrims to help them in love?   Is it our earnest
desire to be a blessing to others?   If this is not the case we have
ourselves grown weary.   All quarrelling among believers is a
sign of spiritual slackness.   Instead of our making use of all our
energies in the front line of battle, the enemy has succeeded in
getting "agents" of his demoniac power behind our lines and
these inspire divisions amongst us, so that valuable energy is
spent in this battle dealing with the "partisans" behind the front
lines.

How can all this be overcome?—this faint condition without
victory can never be the normal state of a sound Christian!

Here only continual reformation can help—only an ever
renewed and fresh vision of Christ, only keener devotion and
increased practical surrender of our life to our Lord.   "Let us
look unto Jesus!"

II.   Quickening Powers

"Therefore lift up the hands which hang down, and the feeble
(lit., paralysed) knees."

The picture at the beginning of our chapter is perhaps still
valid.   One cannot "run" in the arena of faith, "pursue"
and press on to the goal of sanctification—as in the very next
verses we are called to do—if our knees are feeble and our
hands hang down.   For "wrestling matches" require strong
hands, and "athletic races" demand knees which do not grow
tired.

Thus a real and manly renewal of strength in the power of
God is required.   With verve, indeed even with rhythm, is this

brought out in the poetical language of the verse in which this
renewal is demanded.   The author of this passage becomes quite
poetical in his exhortation, clothing it in the original language
in the form of a Greek hexameter.   As with a clarion trumpet
call he wakes up the sleepers and the lingerers:

> And make straight paths for your feet,
> Lest that which is lame be turned out of the way,
> But let it rather be healed.

Looking unto Jesus gives us renewed *freshness*.   The fatigue
disappears.   The paralysis is overcome.   Those who have
strayed from the way or who are wounded are "healed" (Heb.
12: 12, 13).   New courage and confidence fills our souls.   We
get the right standard to estimate our troubles.   We do take
them seriously; but we no longer overestimate them.   Over-
estimation of difficulties is always a sign of fatigue.   But looking
unto Jesus brings strength.   Only from His hand can we receive
the true yard-stick.   After all, the extent of our sufferings is
not appointed and destined by the enemy but by the Lord.
Golgotha proves that God loves us, and should not God, who
did not spare His only begotten Son, give us with Him all
things? (Rom. 8: 32).   Thus we gain new courage, and looking
away to the great Immanuel, the eternal "God with us," who
suffered for us on the cross and won the victory, we receive new
joy, and we experience the truth of the prophet's word: "The
Lord thy God in the midst of thee is mighty" or, literally translated: "Jehovah, thy God, is in thy midst, a saving hero-warrior."
"Light is sown for the righteous, and gladness for the upright in
heart" (Psa. 97: 11).

Looking unto Jesus gives us *peacefulness and fellowship*.   All
strife wears us out.   Conflicts between the redeemed rob us of
our verve.   All self-seeking controversy about things of but
illusory value consumes spiritual energy.   This is the connexion
between the necessity to overcome all signs of fatigue and the
exhortation: "Follow (pursue) peace with all men" (Heb.
12: 14).

By the word "follow on, pursue eagerly" (Gk. *diokete*) the
writer of *Hebrews* resumes the picture of the race from the
beginning of the chapter.   Paul uses this same word twice in
Philippians 3, where he describes the Christian life as a holy

race in such detail as he does in no other portion of his epistles:
"*I press on! . . . I press on!* (Gk. *dioko . . . dioko*) toward the goal
unto the prize" (vv. 12–14). Just as Paul in Philippians 3, had
in view the *final* end, the heavenly prize, so the writer of *Hebrews*
regards here the leading of a life of peace with all men as an
immediate object necessary to reaching that final object. "The
believer is to be as zealous in walking in peace as the racer is to
secure the crown. In a world marked by greed and contention
this is indeed a strenuous affair. It will not be obtained hap-
hazard, but only by such as pursue it as an all-worthy, all-
desirable object, and who make every sacrifice to secure it" (G.
H. Lang).

Difficulties amongst believers can always be overcome. Looking unto the Reconciler makes us conciliatory. There is no time
to quarrel but rather to love. "Let us look unto Jesus."

"Peace" is here classed together with sanctification. "Pursue peace with all men, and the sanctification without which no
man shall see the Lord." Striving after peace brings with it a
right attitude towards our *fellow-men*, striving after holiness a
right attitude towards *God*. Peace gives unity and fellowship
here *below*; holiness arises out of fellowship with the Lord who
is *above*. Both are indispensable. But neither peace nor
sanctification are to be won without effort and diligence. Both
are attained only by steadfast "running." Therefore: "Press
on!"

"Peace," in the full meaning of the Biblical word, is more
than mere absence of strife. Peace is harmony, inward working
together, being tuned in to one another, heart fellowship, love.

The church was born out of eternal love. She owes her life
to the act of love on Golgotha. She lives *by* love and is therefore
also ordained to live *in* love. Love is one-mindedness, a desire
for fellowship, the highest form of inward unity and heart-felt
oneness. Where this love does not exist, all outward formal
unity is mere self-deception and lifeless pretence.

We believe in the one holy, universal church. There is one
foundation—the sacrifice of Golgotha; there is one power of God
in her—the indwelling of the Holy Spirit. There is one object
and goal—the rapture and the perfecting. There is one Lord
and Master—Jesus Christ, our common Redeemer. Therefore
we must also be of one mind in our attitude of love, and, regard-
less of all the differences amongst us, we must find the way of
peace with each other. We must cultivate practical unity, offer

one another the right hand of fellowship and receive one another as Christ received us.

Loving is, however, not simply "loving at a distance" by means of which one imagines oneself to be in fellowship with all the world, but at the same time forgetting to seek the brother who is one's neighbour. This notion of love is very nebulous. We must guard against thinking more of the absent ones than those who are present with us.

Love is not simply a "denominational affair." It is not enough to be enthusiastic for showing unity and fellowship between the various circles of believers, but at the same time not being able to have real fellowship with the individual child of God. Love is nothing sentimental or merely a matter of feeling. It is not something vague and indefinite, but something very real. Love is *will*, is practical action, is the purposeful energy of God, is the manifestation of God's world in the midst of the world here below.

Love seeks the brother. Love believes in the work of Christ in his soul, and we must humble ourselves deeply and, in repentance before God and men, confess that we have often been too slow in this seeking of our brother, and that, with all our faith in God, in this sense we have often been too unbelieving in our belief.

Love is able to bury old strife between brethren. Love can forget the dark past and make a new start. Love kills, in the power of the life of God, all fatal division. Love is the soul of all peace and fellowship amongst believers. Love brings together. Love unites the hearts and leads to fellowship in work at home and abroad, in our own assemblies and churches as well as on the mission-field. Love leads to combined effort in order to reach the great aims of God.

Every one of your fellow-men is to be compared to a mirror. He reflects what is confronting or shining upon him. Every unkindness on your part causes a shadow on his face, even if only for a second; but every act of love brings out brightness in the expression of his countenance, and this brightness will shine back into your own heart. "Through service to joy!"—this word of old "Father Bodelschwingh" may well be engraved in our own hearts, wills, and souls.

Love and service are forces which draw hearts nearer together. People who are cold always feel cold; people who are warm-hearted create a warm atmosphere around them. In what sort of a relationship do you stand to your surroundings? Do you feel yourself being treated coldly or warmly by the others? Seek to a great extent in your own heart the reason for the answer to this question.

Our pursuit of peace and holiness enables us at the same time to serve others. Here again the relationships in the Biblical text are very clear and deep: "Pursue peace with all men, and the sanctification . . . *looking diligently lest any man fall short of the grace of God*" (Heb. 12: 14, 15). Only he who strives after holiness, and tries to live in harmony with his neighbours, has the authority and capacity to serve others. Only service which is done in this attitude of mind has any chance of being fruitful. And this leads to a further consideration.

Looking unto Jesus brings new *commissions*. Our eyes begin to see the needs and distresses round about us. We recognize our responsibility that we should be active in helping those around us in so far as they have become feeble, tired, and paralysed. We begin to see the necessity and possibility of mutual brotherly care and discipline. Looking to the greatest proof of love which ever has been given by love in the history of the whole universe, opens our eyes to the necessity, the privilege, and the many opportunities of ourselves giving practical proofs of watchful love and selfless service in mutual spiritual and bodily care for one another. Looking unto Jesus gives us a new outlook upon the world. It opens our eyes. "Look diligently!" "Lift up the hands which hang down and the feeble knees!"

In the context it is obvious that not so much the hands and knees of the *readers* themselves are meant, as if they are exhorted to make a fresh decision in order to get new freshness and life, but it speaks of the hands and knees of *others*. The readers are expected to be a help for the reviving of these *others*, "that that which is lame be not turned out of the way; but rather be healed . . . Strengthen ye the weak hands and confirm the feeble knees. *Say to them* that are of a fearful heart, Be strong! Fear not!" This passage, taken from the prophets and here quoted in *Hebrews*, is the background of our exhortation (Isa. 35: 3, 4).

There may be many in your neighbourhood who are spiritually lame and weary. Keep in mind that you ought to be the means in God's hands of their restoration and revival. Do not pass by their external and internal need. Your eyes ought to see their dangers. Looking unto Jesus sharpens our eyesight concerning the distresses of our brethren. "Look carefully lest there be any man that falleth short of the grace of God; lest any root of bitterness springing up trouble you, and thereby the many be defiled; lest there be any fornicator or profane person, as Esau" (Heb. 12: 15, 16). "Let us consider one another to provoke unto love and good works" (Heb. 10: 24).

In this spirit of love let us become active Christians. We must awake from our sleep of pious self-centred idleness. It is not enough to affirm the commandment of God with mere feelings. Our Christian life must have muscles. Our strength must become evident in everyday life. God and the world want to see actions.

But work costs effort. He who shuns the heat of the day is no workman. The man who only sits on the spectator's seat will never become victor. During the race in the arena all our energy must be mobilized. Even in ordinary human life it is a true saying, "What is worth doing at all is worth doing well." Work that we do for others but that does not cost us anything, is scarcely worth doing. Thus Scripture says that we should give "all diligence" (II Pet. 1: 10), that we should fight, do battle, pursue after, and press forward (cf. Phil 3: 12), that we should put forth the "labour of love," that we should be "zealous of good works" (Titus 2: 14). Idlers are a ubiquitous people. There are many lazy spectators and passive critics, but "the labourers are few," says the Lord (Matt. 9: 37). And what sort of a person are you, my reader? Are you a labourer or a spectator? Are you an active fighter or a mere onlooker?

Work requires self-denial. Many are quite willing to be active for Christ and His interests as long as it involves no self-sacrifice. This kind of service has in reality no true value: "For whosoever will save his life shall lose it" (Matt. 16: 25). Only those who sow with tears will reap with joy (Psa. 126: 5). We can easily do light work, work which does not cost us any effort, or pain, or sacrifice; but if this is our only work for Christ we need not be surprised if at the great harvest-home we shall appear with empty hands.

The aim, however, of this mutual spiritual love and care is not merely the recovery of the individual but the preservation and protection of the whole. This is the meaning of the words: "Lest any root of bitterness springing up trouble you, and thereby the many (= the majority) be defiled." This does not mean that this mutual shepherding will hinder bitter feelings arising in the heart of the individual—although this, of course, can and

should be attained where such spiritual mutual care is present—
but the author means here apparently *persons* whom he calls
"roots." He is referring in a free type of translation to a word
of the Old Testament law, well-known to his Jewish readers
(Deut. 29: 18).

In this passage Moses warns of the danger of there being
"among you man, or woman, or family, or tribe, whose heart
turneth away from the Lord . . . lest there should be among you
a root that beareth gall and wormwood." And it might even
happen that a man who is such a "root" would feel very self-
confident and say in his heart, "I shall have peace" (Deut. 29: 19),
but God will not forgive and will not spare him: "The anger of
Jehovah and His jealousy shall smoke against that man" (vv.
19, 20). The relationship between the text in *Hebrews*, speaking
of the "root of bitterness," and that in Deuteronomy, speaking
of the "root that beareth gall and wormwood" is obvious. Both
passages speak of *persons* who, although living within the people
of God, turn away from God and become a spiritual hindrance
and a stumbling-block to their fellow-Christians. Thus it is a
matter not so much of certain feelings in the *soul*-life of the individual but rather of the individual *himself* as a *person* and a member of a fellowship.

It is easily possible that a member of the people of God fails
and "comes short of the grace of God" and exercises a harmful
influence upon the others, so that he infects his surroundings
like a "plant with bitter sap and bitter fruits." Thus a Christian
who lives in an unspiritual state of heart, poisons God's vineyard,
the church, like a root that bears gall and wormwood. Apparently the author has in mind the picture of a poisonous plant or
rather of a plant infected with a ruinous disease, which, when it
is mature, harms everything around it. Every failure of an
individual is a twofold danger, not only to himself but also to
others, because his sin might cause these others also to fall. A
single member of the church can, if he is given over to sin and
allowed to go on with it, exercise such a dreadful influence on
the whole circle that the many individuals which make up this
fellowship become defiled by sin. This should be prevented by
mutual spiritual care. Thus shepherding the individual soul is
at the same time a preservation and help for the whole community.

And in this you must see quite clearly that it is therefore possible for yourself to become such a "root of bitterness." Grow-

ing weary in spiritual life is an infectious illness. Through the bitter fruit which arises in your life, poison and weeds can be sown in the lives of others. Either you are a help to your environment or a hindrance. Either you lift up the others or you weigh them down, either you further sanctification or you are a seed of defilement. Some kind of influence always radiates from us, even if unconsciously. Either you are "salt of the earth" or you may become "pepper for the world," either useful or annoying, either a fruit-tree or a poisonous plant, either a channel of blessing or a means of harm.

On the other hand if you devote yourself to holy service for others, you may be sure that being a blessing to others brings blessing to yourself. If we work for the revival of others we are ourselves revived. You will overcome the signs of fatigue in yourself if you give yourself up wholly to the Lord to be commissioned by Him to overcome paralysis and feebleness in others. He who loves and nurses his Ego makes himself spiritually old. Selfishness makes weary. The service of love keeps us young.

Further, looking unto Jesus brings with it new spiritual *initiative and power of resolution*. Let us note the clear *commands*: "Lift up!... Make straight paths!... Pursue peace!" (Heb. 12: 12–14). To own a Bible involves effort. Hearing God's Word imposes obligations. Perhaps many of us need new devotion. One does not overcome weariness by remaining weary. We must "awake" from our sleep (Eph. 5: 14). We must respond to God's call. There must be a new turn towards a more definite attitude of faith and increased active faithfulness. In this deep spiritual sense of the word, we must personally return to "that which was from the beginning," that is Christ Himself (I John 1: 1).

It is true that mere good intentions will not help us very far. How often we have become bankrupt! But the Scripture says clearly that "with purpose of heart" we should cleave to the Lord (Acts 11: 23). Such Spirit-wrought purposes of heart are required. For devotion is not something which God does in our stead, but it has to be done on our part. Christ devoted Himself in order that we should follow His steps and in like manner devote ourselves to God. "I sanctify Myself that they themselves also may be sanctified in truth" (John 17: 19). It may be necessary that we get alone with God and ourselves, bow our knees in prayer, and re-dedicate in a practical sense our life and will to the Lord. This is not, of course, a "second conversion." For conversion in the sense of new birth is an act which takes place once and for all in our life and remains the basis for our whole later spiritual development. But it is a new Spirit-wrought declaration of our will to live in purer and deeper sanctification.

And is it not a fact that even after our new birth we have often become lukewarm, superficial, and weary to such an extent that the great things of our great God, as the all overpowering and all overshadowing realities, no longer overwhelm us? Have we not also often experienced the fact that the mere acknowledgment of weaknesses and shortcomings did not themselves produce progress? Perhaps we have been *too* afraid of making "good resolutions" and have therefore not had the spiritual energy to come to a holy "purpose of heart" (Acts 11: 23) and thus to make a new start by a definite act of personal devotion. Spiritual awakening and remaining fresh do not come automatically or by magic. No, you must yourself act—not of course in a dead, legal manner, but *definitely*, in faith. Start again to serve your Redeemer and Lord anew and faithfully. Deny yourself and bear witness to Him. Then *continue!* You will yourself advance experimentally: one learns prayer *by* praying, witnessing *by* witnessing, serving *by* serving, helping *by* helping. And your life will become fresher. Your days will become useful, and your heart happy.

You yourself must, however, *really desire* this and give to it your whole will without any reservation (Rev. 22: 17). The Bible says nowhere that the will of man must be "broken." Such expressions sound very devoted and humble and are, no doubt, meant sincerely by those who use them, but in reality no one is helped by such unscriptural terms—neither believers nor those who are willing to believe, and certainly not the opposers or despisers of the Christian faith. What Scripture shows is that it is not the "will" which has to be broken but rather the egocentric "*self*-will," not our personal energy, but rather man's rebellion against God. As to the will itself, the regulation principle is that it has to be brought into line with the will of God. Our will should certainly remain "will," but has only by the power of the Holy Spirit to will what God wills. And just in this "willing of the will of God" it will become a real and strong will, that is, a powerful energy of a true personality. As long as it remained "self-will" it was not really a will at all, but merely a plaything in the hands of the mighty power of sin which oppressed and forced it to do *its* will (Rom. 7: 19, 20). At the highest estimate, it was only a striving, a searching, a wishing, and a yearning—for sin degrades and enervates us. But in Christ we awaken to ourselves. In Him alone do we become "personalities" in the real God-planned sense of the word. Only by subjecting ourselves to the Lord of Lords, do we creatures receive a real "will."

Also in the life of the church as a whole all signs of fatigue must be overcome. It is a fact which almost regularly repeats itself in the history of the people of God that every new generation of the church is accompanied by a crisis. Very often the third generation especially of a spiritual movement has failed. It has so often given up spiritual energies and Biblical truths and convictions which by the pioneers of their movement, the fathers of earlier revivals, had been held to be precious and holy. One can recognize this in Old Testament history. "And the people served Jehovah all the days of Joshua [first generation], and all the days of the elders that outlived Joshua [second generation] who had seen all the great work of Jehovah that He had wrought for Israel. . . . And also all that generation were gathered unto their fathers: and there arose another [the third] generation after them which knew not Jehovah, nor yet the works which He had done for Israel . . . and they forsook the Lord the God of their fathers . . . and followed other gods" (Judges 2: 7, 10, 12). How very grave! Let us not lull ourselves to sleep in false security. No group of Christians, whether arising out of State church or Free church, whether organized or unorganzied, has any guarantee of retaining the freshness and vigour which it had at its beginning. Every new generation in the local churches as well as in spiritual movements in general must "lay hold" (I Tim. 6: 12) afresh for themselves, quite directly, personally and individually, of the blessings which had been received and held fast by their spiritual fathers. Spiritual possessions cannot be merely "inherited."

The letter to the Hebrews itself grew out of the crisis connected with the arising of a new generation. The letter is a warning and an appeal by the Spirit of God to that second generation to hold fast the confession in witness and life of the first generation.

A "crisis" need not of necessity be a "catastrophe." Trials

are opportunities for victories. The ever-available power of the omnipresent Christ, which never grows old, is at hand for new times and new people.

This is at the same time the meaning of the well-known verse, "Jesus Christ is the same yesterday and today, yea and for ever" (Heb. 13: 8). This word should be read in connexion with Heb. 11 and 12, and in relationship to its own context. It had just been said: "Remember them that had the rule over you, who spake unto you the word of God, and considering the issue of their life, imitate their faith" (v. 7). Immediately after this text follows that radiant word dealing with the ever-living, mighty, Divine Lord of all times and all history.

This means: Men and women are called away. Generations sink into the grave. The leaders of past generations are no longer here. *But Christ remaineth.* In the midst of the coming and going of the generations He is the rock of His church. He is far above all changes in situations and persons. He is the One Who binds the generations together. He is the living link between "yesterday" and "today" in the history of His people, the connexion between each generation at any given time and all generations before and after. He is the Head who unites all the redeemed through the generations past, present, and future. So He is the living, personal uniting principle of the church. This is true from the view-point of the contemporary "horizontal" *cross*-sections of the church, that is, of each generation living simultaneously in all parts of the earth. It is also true from the view-point of the "vertical" *longitudinal* sections of the church's history, that is, throughout the successive centuries and generations forming the entire development of the church from the day of its founding to its completion, rapture, and perfecting at His coming. This means that in spite of all individual changes in detail, the spiritual essence of the life of the church remains in Christ unchanged throughout all generations. The death of the heroes of faith, those forerunners, leaders, and examples (Heb. 13: 7, 17, 24), does not cause the slightest loss in the essence of the life and faith of the people of God. Even though the teachers go, the teaching remains the same. It is true, as I read on John Wesley's tomb in Westminster Abbey, that "God buries His labourers but His labour and work goes on." Therefore, do not grow weary! The Lord is ever present.

Years ago I visited in Stuttgart the widow of the well-known German Christian writer, Professor Bettex. In the study of this

brave confessor of Christ I saw a picture which Professor
Bettex had painted himself. It represented a rock in the midst
of the wildest waves. The waves are represented as surging
mightily against this rock. But they flow back broken and
smashed.

Friedrich Bettex was an author who helped thousands of his
readers by his numerous apologetic works, which were most
reliable in their many scientific statements, Biblically sound, and
deeply impressive and persuasive in their witness to Christ. By
this picture he wished to show the main object of his own life:
In the midst of time stands Christ, the Rock of Ages. The
billows of doubt and the waves of hatred of God and Christ surge
against Him, but it is the waves that are broken. He, the Rock,
is unmoved.

Thus Christ gives His own the victory. One can throw His
servants in this world into prison; one can banish them to scorch-
ing deserts or freezing steppes. They are "stoned, sawn asunder,
tempted" (Heb. 11: 37). But their experience will always be the
same as that of the men in the fiery furnace: One is with them who
comes down from heaven and who is able to keep them from
hurt and harm, in any case inwardly, though He does not always
do so outwardly (Dan. 3: 20–27). "They looked unto Him and
were lightened" (Psa. 34: 5). "In all these things we are more
than conquerors through Him that loved us" (Rom. 8: 37).

This encourages us greatly. It should be also a holy stimulus
and incentive. For if Christ our Saviour is such a firm rock,
our hearts also should be strong and firm (Heb. 13: 9). Christ
will never forsake His people. Therefore His people must never
forsake Him. The younger generation especially must take this
to heart. Faithfulness for faithfulness! The "today" of the
church is under obligation on account of its "yesterday," and
both are under obligation because of the faithfulness of Christ,
who was and is "the same yesterday, and today, yea and for
ever."

This is the reason why the words about the bygone human
leaders and the eternally living Saviour (Heb. 13: 7, 8) are immediately followed by the exhortation and encouragement: "For it
is good that the heart be established by grace" (v. 9).

The homecall of faithful servants of God brings with it a holy
obligation for all those who remain behind.

Our life is short. Our days fly by. Earthly things are not
the real things. That which really matters lies somewhere else,

not in time, but in eternity, not in that which passes by, but in that which remains, not in the past or the present, but in the future. Thus we must press forward with a serious turn of mind and yet inwardly comforted, not trusting in ourselves and yet full of courage, not looking at our own powerlessness but looking to Christ's victorious power. "Therefore seeing we have this ministry, even as we have obtained mercy, we faint not" (II Cor. 4: 1).

When Abraham at the end of his life wanted to win a bride for his son Isaac, he sent the eldest of his servants to his relatives in Mesopotamia. Then, before leaving, this servant asked him: "Peradventure the woman will not be willing to follow me unto this land [Canaan]: must I needs bring thy son again unto the land whence thou camest?" (Gen. 24: 5). Abraham answered— and in the Bible report one can feel and sense the energy of his will and the strength of his emotions and sentiments—"*Beware thou* that thou bring *not* my son *thither again!* and if the woman be not willing to follow thee, then thou shalt be clear from this my oath: only thou shalt *not* bring my son *thither again!*" (Gen. 24: 6, 8).

"Not thither again!" "Beware thou!" "Not thither again!" These three expressions show the intensity of the decision and the feelings of the Patriarch. The father of faith demands of the coming generations the practical recognition of the irrevocability of the patriarchal call. What the first generation has attained in faith must never be given up by the second or third generations. The children must show themselves worthy of the attitude and devotion of their spiritual fathers. The following generation should faithfully administer the inheritance of their forefathers in the faith.

We often deplore—and unfortunately often rightly so—that the people of God in our time show so little of being really alive and keen for Christ. We recognize that we are lacking the spirit of revival and that the last twenty years of the last century and the first ten years of the present century, generally speaking, saw more of the powerful working of the Holy Spirit. In those times many more people awoke out of their sleep of sin than today. There were leaders and shepherds in private and public Christian life in a measure unknown today. We think of the times of Finney, Moody, Torrey, Baedeker, George Müller, Spurgeon, and many others. But with all this recognition and regret perhaps we remain ourselves unchanged. Our yearning

and desire may be honest, but is apparently not Spirit-filled
enough. We wait, and probably also pray, for the Lord to send
a revival. And in the last analysis it begins to appear as though
God were the real cause of there being no wide spread revival,
simply because He does not answer our prayers.

And yet the situation is really quite different!

Nowhere is it taught in the Bible that we should *wait* for a
revival. Revivals must be! But the children of God have not
to take up a *waiting* attitude towards them. Never does Holy
Scripture place the emphasis on practical holiness and on witnessing in the *future*, either near or distant. It brings us a *present*
Christ, a Saviour who desires to make our life fruitful and to fill
us with power *today* and *now*. For if the revival were to come
only after some years' time (God grant that it may come sooner)
what should we be doing in the meantime? No, we dare not
forget the "today." The past exists in our memory, the future
in our expectancy; what we *possess* is the *present*. Mastering
the ever-present moment means mastering life. And if you do
not serve the Lord *today* there is no guarantee that you will serve
Him *tomorrow*.

The King's business is urgent. What we can do today, let us
not put off till tomorrow. If the Spirit incites us today to
witness for the Lord in order to win a soul for Him, let us
obey *today*. When tomorrow comes the enemy will certainly
have found a thousand new reasons why we should not follow the voice of God. It belongs to true service to God that
we should have a heart and mind clearly determined to do God's
will *today*. "Whatsoever thy hand findeth to do, do it with
thy might" (Eccles. 9: 10). "Go, work *today* in the vineyard"
(Matt. 21: 28).

Then new blessings will come. When you yourself have been
awakened, you will be able to wake up others, and so small
circles of spiritually awakened Christians will arise, little cells
from which the light can be spread further. You should belong
to such. The Lord wants to use *you*, even though perhaps, in
the sight of man, you may not have a conspicuous position,
simply because God wishes you to do in obscurity a hidden and
quiet service. In eternity you will be surprised that God could
effect so much through your life only because it was really devoted
to Christ, revived and remaining full of life till the goal was
reached. That is God's will. Therefore it must be your will
and decision also, and this just now and today.

We read in the life-story of Isaac: "And Isaac digged again the wells of water, which they had digged in the days of Abraham his father; for the Philistines had stopped them after the death of Abraham: And he called their names after the names by which his father had called them" (Gen. 26: 18).

This is spiritually our situation. Our fathers in the faith digged "wells" and named them with names. The well of the word of God, the well of prayer, the well of fellowship of the saints, the well of happy witnessing, the well of missionary service—all these were heavenly springs from which they drew water and which kept their personal life of faith fresh, as well as the life of their churches.

But the first generation has been called away and the "Philistines" have come—sin, worldliness, strife among brethren, lukewarmness, lack of interest in God's word and work, cowardice in witness, want of sacrifice and missionary spirit—and the "wells" of the fathers have been stopped. Withering of the life of faith, lack of prayer and unfruitfulness in witness, spiritual stagnation in church life, subjection under the bondage of human tradition, narrowness of horizon, are the consequences.

What shall we do?

We must dig again the wells of the fathers. We must learn to pray again as our fathers prayed. We must bear witness as they did. We must sacrifice for the spread of the word of God and for missionary service as they used to do. We must love the brethren as they loved and practised the fellowship of the saints. We must listen afresh to God's Word and open our hearts to the working of the Holy Spirit. Our place in church or chapel must not be empty. Our contribution towards church and mission-work must always be given with readiness of heart. Our prayers must be regular and sincere. Our mouth must not be silent. We must witness for Christ and be soul-winners just as the former generations of believers, who, in spite of failures and short-comings which, of course, had been in their lives as in ours, had yet seen the mighty deeds of God.

"Isaac" must dig again "Abraham's" wells. Then new water of life will flow in our churches, and this promise of Scripture will be fulfilled in an ever deeper, richer degree:

"And the Lord shall guide thee continually, and satisfy thy soul in dry places and make strong thy bones; and thou shalt be like a watered garden, and like a spring of water, whose waters fail not. And they that shall be of thee shall build the old waste places: thou shalt raise up the foundations of many generations; and thou shalt be called, The repairer of the breach, The restorer of paths to dwell in" (Isa. 58: 11, 12).

Therefore once again: "Lift up the hands which hang down! Make straight paths! Press on!"

In the arena of faith:

"*Let us look unto Jesus.*"

CHAPTER VII

WASTED PRIVILEGES

"Looking carefully . . . lest there be any fornicator, or profane person, as Esau, who for one mess of meat sold his own birthright [Lit. his firstborn rights]. For ye know how that even when he afterward desired to inherit the blessing, he was rejected: (for he found no place of repentance), though he sought it [the blessing] diligently with tears" (Heb. 12: 16, 17).

HIGH, indeed, is the standing conferred in New Testament salvation; deep, however, can be the downfall. Therefore in every sound Christian life to joy must be added seriousness, to thankfulness responsibility, to confidence carefulness. For this reason there are so many warnings in *Hebrews*. One of the most impressive is that with reference to Esau.

"Look carefully . . . lest there be . . . any profane person, as Esau, who for one mess of meat sold his own birthright. For ye know how that even when he afterward desired to inherit the blessing, he was rejected (for he found no place of repentance) [*i.e.* change of mind, altering of his father's decision, cancelling, annulment], though he sought it [the blessing, by means of a change of his father's decision] diligently with tears" (Heb. 12: 16, 17).

Esau was the firstborn of Isaac. The writer of this letter is drawing the attention of his readers to their privileges, their responsibilities, and their dangers by referring to Esau's behaviour and its outcome. The chief object of this reference is to warn them. But the full weight of this warning is felt only through consideration of Esau's original high position.

The first readers of *Hebrews* knew well, as Jews by birth, what were the privileges of the firstborn son. The term is used in the New Testament as a picture of the high position of honour of the members of the church of Christ, indeed of Christ Himself. *In the context of Hebrews 12 the full possession and enjoyment of the heavenly privilege of the firstborn is the equivalent of the victor's prize in the race, when the runner in the arena of faith shall have reached the glorious goal.*

Pre-eminently and in a quite unique manner it is CHRIST Who is the Firstborn. This glory of His radiates from the New Testament revelation in a threefold way.

He is "the Firstborn of all creation" (Col. 1: 15). This is His position of honour as seen from the *past*, Christ, being the "Firstborn" from the beginning, as "son" before and above all creatures.

He is "the Firstborn from the dead" (Col. 1: 18; Rev. 1: 5). This is His position of honour in the *present*, which He holds as the Risen One Who possesses the "pre-eminence" as "Head" of His body, the church.

He is "the Firstborn among many brethren" (Rom. 8: 29). This will be His position of honour in the eternal *future* when He shall be revealed as the glorified Redeemer of His glorified redeemed (Heb. 1: 6).

Thus the New Testament witness to Christ as the Firstborn refers to all the three periods of time during the whole course of the history of salvation. It shows Him at the same time as the highest dignitary in all spheres of Divine revelation: in the kingdom of creation, in the kingdom of redemption, in the kingdom of perfection. Wherever we look, Christ is the Firstborn. "Let us look unto Jesus!"

Furthermore, the word "firstborn" is used in order to express the special position of grace of the CHURCH. So the letter to the Hebrews, after having spoken of the "birthright" of Esau and having drawn certain conclusions from it for New Testament readers, adds only a few sentences later: "Ye have come . . . to the church of the firstborn [ones] who are enrolled in heaven" (Heb. 12: 22, 23). And James in his epistle declares: "Of His own will He brought us forth by the word of truth, that we should be a kind of firstfruits of His creatures" (James 1: 18).

Both these letters were in the first place addressed to Jewish Christian readers. Thus the word "birthright" must be explained and understood by reference to its Old Testament sense.

The chief emphasis lies not so much on the order of birth with respect to time but rather to rank and dignity. Otherwise it would not be possible (which however the Old Testament in fact does) to speak of a man being "made" the "firstborn" at a time long after his birth. "He shall cry unto Me, Thou art my father, my God, and the rock of my salvation! I also will *make* him my Firstborn, the highest of the kings of the earth" (Psa. 89: 26–28). And in the reverse sense it would not be possible for one who, from the view-point of time, was born as the first son, to lose this birthright at some later occasion under given circumstances (*cf.* Reuben: I Chron. 5: 1, 2, and Esau).

The fact that the essential idea of being "firstborn" is priority of rank, not accident of birth, is shown also in I Chron. 26: 10. This passage mentions that of a certain family of Levites one of the sons, called Shimri, was the chief, for "though he was not the firstborn yet his father made him chief." Also here the underlying principle is that in regular cases the firstborn would have been the chief and thus possess the priority of rank. The same truth is the force of Col. 1: 15. There Paul says that Christ is "the Firstborn of all creation", not meaning that He was the first in time to be born and so had a beginning, but that He has the pre-eminence as the Ruler of the whole universe.

The word for "birthright" is, in the text of *Hebrews*, in the plural (Gk. *ta prototokia*, neuter plural). Also in the Septuagint, the Greek translation of the Old Testament, the word for "birthright," used in Gen. 25: 31, 34, is a plural term. This indicates that the blessing of the birthright is a plurality. It should be rendered "the rights of the firstborn." According to the social order of the Old Testament, and also from the view-point of the general history of salvation, this blessing is threefold:

> position of authority,
> priestly service,
> a double portion of the inheritance.

I. The Rights of the Firstborn in Israel

1. *The position of authority.* After the father, the firstborn was the representative of authority in the family. He was "lord" over his younger brothers (*cf.* Gen. 27: 37). Thus David's eldest brother "commanded" David his younger brother to go to a family sacrifice to Bethlehem, which fact even king Saul and his son Jonathan were expected to acknowledge as a sufficient reason for David not appearing at even the king's table, in spite of the fact that he had been invited and ought to attend (I Sam. 20: 27, 29). At table the sons of an Israelitic household sat according to age and rank, "the firstborn according to his birthright and the youngest according to his youth" (Gen. 43: 33; *cf.* also Gen. 48: 14, 17–19).

2. *Priestly service.* At the same time the above-mentioned incident from the life of David shows that the eldest brother, the "firstborn" of the family, saw to the ordering of the family sacrifice, that is, he had to act as household priest. Above all, moreover, the great general lines and governing connexions in the Old Testament and in the universal history of salvation show that birthright and priesthood belong together.

According to the plan of God, Israel should have become God's "firstborn" among the nations (Ex. 4: 22). At the same time Israel was appointed to be God's own possession from among all peoples, "a kingdom of priests, and a holy nation" (Ex. 19: 5, 6). As God's reaction to the outrage of Pharaoh, who intended to wipe out Israel and thus destroy God's "firstborn son," it was determined by God that the firstborn of Egypt, man and beast, should be destroyed. "Thus saith Jehovah, Israel is My son, My firstborn . . . and thou hast refused to let him go: behold, I will slay thy son, thy firstborn" (Ex. 4: 22, 23).

Because God then spared the Israelite firstborn at the passover He ordered that every Jewish firstborn male was to be regarded as dedicated to Him in a special sense. Thus dedication to Jehovah and the birthright of the firstborn, including duties and privileges, were fundamentally bound up with one another. And to possess the birthright meant that one was at the same time separated unto holy service, that is, for the priesthood. After the worship of the golden calf in the wilderness, and as reward for the uncompromising attitude of the tribe of Levi on the side of God (Ex. 32: 26-29), God transferred to the tribe of Levi this portion of dedication and priesthood which up to that time had been the obligation and privilege of every Israelite firstborn son. "For all the firstborn of the children of Israel are Mine . . . on the day that I smote every firstborn in the land of Egypt I sanctified them for Myself. And I have taken the Levites *instead of* all the firstborn of the children of Israel . . . to do the service of the children of Israel in the tent of meeting [tabernacle]" (Num. 8: 17-19; 3: 12, 44, 45).

This is the general and special historical presupposition and connexion in revealed history of the calling of the tribe of Levi to the priesthood. In the background of this special election of Levi there stands the national position of Israel as God's firstborn son, as well as the fundamental relationship between birthright and ordination to the priesthood. But also after this special calling of Levi there remained a certain kind of house and

family priesthood of every firstborn Israelite, even though the
service in the temple was the exclusive duty of Levi.

The third blessing of the birthright was:

3. *A double portion of the inheritance.* According to the clear
instructions laid down in the book of Deuteronomy, the Israelite
father had to give to his firstborn, no matter what the family
circumstances were in detail, "a *double* portion of all that he hath:
for he is the beginning of his strength; the right of the firstborn
is his" (Deut. 21: 15–17). This means that if, for example, a
father had four sons, his total possessions had to be divided
into five parts and the firstborn received two parts and every
other son one.

Very important developments in the total history of salvation
are connected with and resulting from these three main ordinances of the Israelite birthright.

Among the twelve tribes of Jacob, Reuben owned the birthright. But in spite of this the Messiah is not "the lion of the
tribe of Reuben." For Reuben was divested of the rights of the
firstborn on account of his shameful sin recounted in Gen. 35:
22, and lost therefore also the right of the Messiah coming in his
family: the genealogy is not to be reckoned after the birthright
(I Chron. 5: 1). He was deprived of all privileges and should
"not have the excellency" (Gen. 49: 3, 4). The next following
brothers, Simeon and Levi, were also excluded (Gen. 49: 5–7) on
account of their outrageous deed in Sichem (Gen. 34: 25).

For all these reasons Reuben's privilege of birthright was
divided up as follows:

(*a*) The double portion of the inheritance was given to *Joseph*
and was divided and transferred to his two sons *Ephraim and
Manasseh*, so that each of these received the area of a whole tribal
territory (I Chron. 5: 1). This is the reason why these two, who
were actually only grandsons of Jacob, were thus treated as
though they had been sons of the patriarch, and therefore in
the same way as their father's brothers. As Jacob had ordained:
"Ephraim and Manasseh are mine; as Reuben and Simeon, they
shall be mine" (Gen. 48: 5).

(*b*) The priesthood was given to *Levi*. At the same time by
this means the judgment of dispersion which was inflicted on
Levi (Gen. 49: 5–7), according to which on account of his outrage
in Sichem (Gen. 34: 25), he should receive no defined area in the
Promised Land, was transformed into a blessing, for although

I

this judgment of dispersion was outwardly upheld, Levi's off-spring received 48 cities which were scattered all over the country within reach of every Israelite (Num. 35: 1–7; Josh. 21: 1ff., esp. 41).

(c) The position of authority and rule fell to *Judah*, Jacob's fourth son. "Judah prevailed above his brethren, and of him came the prince" (I Chron. 5: 2). Thus the tribe of Judah became the royal tribe, which at once carried a Messianic significance. "The sceptre shall not depart from Judah, nor the ruler's staff from between his feet, until Shiloh [the hero, Christ] come; and unto Him shall the obedience of the peoples be" (Gen. 49: 10).

In consequence of all these pre-developments, and the corresponding Divine decisions, the Messiah is not "the lion of the tribe of Reuben," as otherwise would have been expected, but "the lion of the tribe of Judah" (Rev. 5: 5).

Also in the future kingdom of God the division and transference of Reuben's birthright will remain unchanged for ever. Christ, the Messianic King, will be out of the house of Judah, the priesthood in Israel will be in the family of Zadok the Levite (Ezek. 48: 11), and Ephraim and Manasseh, the descendants of Joseph, will hold their double portion.

This whole connexion reveals the immense importance of the Israelite privileges of the firstborn. They influenced and shaped the most decisive lines of history in the whole Old Testament development of revelation right on into the New Testament history of salvation and the coming kingdom of God. This is true

> territorially:
> Levi, the priestly tribe, receiving no defined tribal area, but 48 holy cities scattered all over the country;
> politically:
> Judah receiving the kingship and leadership in Israel;
> dynastically:
> the royal house of David coming out of Judah (Matt. 1: 2–7; Luke 3: 31–34);
> prophetically and Messianically:
> Christ the Messiah arising from Judah and not from Reuben or Simeon or Levi.

Thus the Israelite birthright is the God-appointed, historical basis and starting-point not only for temporal, personal, family, and national affairs but also for the realization of universal, indeed, eternal principles in the worship of God, inspiration, prophecy, and the Messianic Kingdom.

II. THE BIRTHRIGHT OF THE CHURCH
The Great Opportunity

Seen from the point of view of the New Testament, all this is symbolic and typical language pointing to the spiritual possessions of the church.   By the church being called the "assembly of the firstborn which is written in heaven" (Heb. 12: 23), in connexion with these Old Testament ordinances of the birthright, a threefold spiritual possession is indicated:

> outstanding and glorious fulness of heavenly blessings,
> spiritual and heavenly priesthood, and
> God-given kingship and rule.

Every thoughtful Jewish Christian reader of the letter to the Hebrews and of the letter of James would clearly recognize this.

That in this Scripture under the term "the firstborn" *men* (not angels or other beings in the spiritual world) are meant, is proved by the additional "whose names are enrolled in heaven" and by reference to the Lord's word to His disciples: "Rejoice because your names are written in heaven" (Luke 10: 20), as well as by Paul describing his fellow-labourers as those "whose names are in the book of life" (Phil. 4: 3).

But as regards this threefold content of the birthright, the New Testament reality far exceeds the Old Testament type.   Everything is much more inclusive, more spiritual, more heavenly.

1.   *The New Testament fulness of blessing.*   Unsearchable are the riches of Christ which are the privilege of the church (Eph. 3: 8, 10).   Its standing is far higher than the standing of Israel as a nation.   The heavenly blessings of the New Testament church exceed all the earthly blessings of the Old Testament covenant people.   The "church of the firstborn" has here indeed a "*double* portion" in blessing, yea, far more than that.   The New Covenant mightily surpasses the Old Covenant (Heb. 8; II Cor. 3). The least in the kingdom of heaven is greater than the greatest under the dispensation of the Law (Matt. 11: 11).   Blessed therefore are our eyes for they see, and our ears for they hear

what prophets and righteous men of Old Testament times did not see or hear (Matt. 13: 16, 17). "Blessed be the God and Father of our Lord Jesus Christ, who has blessed us with every spiritual blessing in the heavenlies [lit.] in Christ" (Eph. 1: 3).

Thus in Christ a salvation has arisen which outshines, as the Sun of Eternity, all previous revelations of God. In Him full salvation is come. All the riches of heaven are opened up. As Saviour, Christ is more than a mere Healer or Physician of soul and body (cf. Luke 4: 23). He is more than a mere Overcomer of spiritual, moral and physical hindrances in individuals and nations. As Saviour and Redeemer He does not merely annul the debts, bringing the "minus" to the point "nought"; He does not merely remove the negative in taking away all damage and loss; but He gives at the same time an overwhelming positive value which a millionfold surpasses the "point nought" and raises us up to overflowing joy of life (Eph. 1: 18; John 10: 10, 11), to inexhaustible rejoicing (Phil. 4: 4), to power to live a victorious life (Rom. 8: 37), to true dignity in our personality (I Pet. 2: 9; Eph. 4: 1), in fact, to everlasting fulfilment of the true nobility of man.

"Salvation," within the meaning of the New Testament, is therefore the same as "the unsearchable riches of Christ" (Eph. 3: 8). It is the sphere of activity of the Risen One, the sum total of His mighty works here below. As Saviour, Christ is the One who brings salvation, the Victor over all powers of darkness, the Sun which radiates all energies for generating new life, the One who brings to us the triumphant, eternal Kingdom of God (John 4: 42; 3: 16; I John 4: 14).

Thus in the explanation of the title "Saviour" it is not enough to consider only the etymological root of the Greek word *soter* from *sozein* (to heal, to make sound, cf. Matt. 9: 21, 22; Mark 5: 23; 6: 56). The etymology of a word is never sufficient to decide its usage and sense. Where healing of the sick is described in the New Testament usually quite another word is used (Gk. *therapeuein*, e.g., Matt. 4: 24; Mark 3: 10, which occurs in over 35 passages in the Gospels). But the Biblical word "Saviour" (*soter*), although including the idea of healing, yet surpasses that meaning.

2. *The New Testament priesthood.* But still more: every one of these "millionaires of heaven" is, according to God's call, a priest of the Highest. "He [Christ] has made us to be a kingdom, to be priests unto His God and Father" (Rev. 1: 6).

What does this involve?

There is a superficial and thoughtless manner of speaking of the general priesthood of the church as though it were already present in a local church when the latter has no appointed minister or ordained pastor to serve it. Whereas the New Testament nowhere declares that the general priesthood is fulfilled in any form of church organization or order of service. On the contrary, a local church may have an ordained minister and yet at the same time exercise in principle the general priesthood. A local church may have general freedom of speech and yet in practice miss the real priesthood of all believers. General priesthood and general freedom of speech are by no means identical. In God's church there exists no general freedom of speech but only freedom of the Spirit, who distributes the gifts and guides as to their administration according to His own will and control.

The expression "general priesthood," in the literal combination of these two words "general" and "priesthood," is not to be found in the Scriptures. It arose during the time of the Reformation in contrast to the distinction between "priests" and "laymen" in the Roman Catholic Church. The Bible speaks of a "royal" priesthood (I Pet. 2: 9; Ex. 19: 6) and of a "holy" priesthood (I Pet. 2: 5).

In opposition to the Roman Catholic system of a special priestly hierarchical caste, the Reformers emphasized the spiritual and positional equality of all true believers in Christ before God and in the church. And quite rightly so. Thus the expression "general priesthood" is correct and certainly Biblical as to its meaning, although not found literally in Scriptures.

Only one must be careful not to interpret it purely negatively, that is, as merely denying clericalism, or regarding it chiefly from the view-point of church organization, order of ministry, and the practice of the preaching of the word—as if the "general priesthood" in its real nature were especially a *negation* of ordaining an appointed minister or local pastor, and an *affirmation* of an undifferentiated equality of all male believers in the church as regards ministry and preaching.

In reality, believing women are just as much included in the general priesthood as believing men, but, of course, each within the sphere given to him or to her by God. *All* should, however, have priestly hearts and minds. Of course, certain practical consequences have to be drawn from this also for the outward form of church meetings and of the ministry of the word. But the centre of gravity of the truth lies much deeper. The general priesthood, as also the guidance of the Holy Spirit, is not a mere privilege and obligation of the gatherings in the local churches. The teaching of all Scripture referring to this subject (Rom. 8: 14; Gal. 5: 18; John 16: 13), makes clear that it has to be applied to our whole life from morning till evening, and every day in the week, not only the Lord's Day. It is certainly not limited to the beginning and ending of church gatherings, such as meetings for worship, Bible reading, or prayer, but includes the whole man, not only in but also outside the meeting-rooms, halls, chapels and church buildings. In this full sense of the word the whole New Testament people of God is "a kingdom of priests and a holy nation" (Ex. 19: 6; I Pet. 2: 5–9).

On the basis of this general priesthood the "spiritual gifts" have to be developed in the church (I Cor. 12–14). This should be practised in each case under the guidance of the Holy Spirit according to the God-ordained commission and endowment of each individual. General priesthood and charismatic leading of the Spirit are therefore to be distinguished from one another (Gk. *charisma* = gift of grace). The former includes the larger circle; the latter is included, as a smaller circle, in the former, thus being only a part of the former. Every redeemed one is called to the general priesthood. But not every New Testament "priest" is a bearer of spiritual gifts for special ministry or Divine service. And even those who are bearers of such gifts of the Spirit are not commissioned in every case and as a matter of course with the exercise of the preaching of the word. Each should stand in every instance under the fresh ordering and leading of the Holy Spirit (I Cor. 12: 4ff.; 14: 26).

From all this it follows that the guidance of the Spirit does not set in only with the beginning of a church gathering. Guidance by the Holy Spirit is not magical, but natural and yet holy, not mechanical but organic, not restricted to special seasons, but all-inclusive of the totality of time and life.

The connexion between the word "Spirit" (Gk. *pneuma*) and "leading" (Gk. *ago, hodegeo*) occurs only three times in the New Testament, and each time it refers to the *total* life of the Christian (Rom. 8: 14; Gal. 5: 18; John 16: 13). It never refers exclusively, nor even chiefly, to the principles of church order or Divine service. It is of course obvious, and included in the claim for the whole of life to be guided by the Spirit, that the gatherings of the church should be led on every occasion by the Spirit of

God. Nor does the Scripture in any passage suggest a graduated difference in church gatherings as if in one kind of meeting there should be more evidence of general priesthood and more leading of the Holy Spirit than in another kind of gathering. No, the Spirit of God claims the *total* man and thus the *total* life of the church. All the time of a Christian, within and without the church life, should be under direct leading from above through the Holy Spirit. Therefore it is also in full accord with the Biblical idea of guidance by the Holy Spirit for a preacher of the Word to prepare himself for his ministry, praying to the Lord to give him the right word and message, in a quiet time of meditation and prayer at home *before* his ministry. In every case, of course, he must remain open for further guidance.

The duties of a priest were fivefold: sacrificial service, prayer, witness, pastoral work (spiritual shepherding), blessing.

In all this we must clearly acknowledge that the general priesthood of the church is not something impersonal, merely objective, especially corporate, as if "the church," only as a "body," an organization or a spiritual organism, is blessed with a priestly position and has to perform holy obligations. No, it is not only "the church" in general, but the individual members who are meant at the same time most emphatically.

The idea that "the church" as such has to do this or that, is to a certain extent related to the basis of the erroneous Roman Catholic conception of a body corporate: "the church" gives men the Bible, "the church" interprets the Scripture, "the church" exercises authority, "the church" spreads the Christian truth in the world.

But the Bible teaches the *personal* responsibility of each *individual* believer. Each single believer has to act himself as a priest of God. We are not allowed to hide our "I" behind the general "We." Otherwise everybody's business will soon become nobody's business, and the practical realization of the general priesthood of the church will be evaporated and become after all an actual failure.

In this sense, that all Christian service is individual, not only corporate, we speak of the general priesthood of the church and its members.

The New Testament priesthood is a holy service of *sacrifice*. The sacrifice on Golgotha of the Lamb of God was, of course, once and for all and can never be repeated (Heb. 10: 10–14). But those who have been purchased for God by means of this sacrifice should be a holy sacrifice themselves in their whole life. "And for their sakes I sanctify [devote] Myself that they also might be sanctified [devoted] through the truth" (John 17: 19).

In the consecration of their whole being and manner of life their priestly rendering of spiritual sacrifices should be made manifest and actually proved, even

in the devotion of their life: Rom. 12: 1;

in the holiness of their deeds: I Pet. 2: 5, 9;

in readiness to help and to be charitable: Heb. 13: 6;

in liberality of contributing gifts for the Lord's work: Phil. 4: 18;

in total dedication of their own persons to the spread of the gospel: Phil. 2: 17; II Tim. 4: 6;

in Spirit-wrought prayer: Rev. 8: 3, 4; Psa. 141: 1, 2;

in triumphant adoration and worship: Heb. 13: 15.

In all these things the Scriptures are very practical. Even the spiritual sacrifices which should be offered by the holy priesthood of the New Testament, according to I Pet. 2: 5, are not sacrifices exclusively in the sphere of the merely inward life, the invisible, intellectual, mental, soulish realm, that is, are not only prayers or thanksgivings or mere feelings and abstract thoughts, but rather "spiritual" in the sense that the word has in the Pauline expression "spiritual gifts" (I Cor. 12: 1). There "spiritual gifts" mean, without a shadow of doubt, "Spirit-*wrought*, Spirit-*led*, Spirit-*saturated*" gifts of grace (I Cor. 12: 4–11). Thus also here the "spiritual" sacrifices are Spirit-*wrought* and Spirit-*filled* deeds of holy service, both the outward and visible as well as the inward and invisible (prayers, supplication, thanksgivings, worship). In the kingdom of God, even money is a *spiritual* matter.

To this spiritual sacrificial service of the church and all its individual members, and thus to the practical exercise of the New Testament general priesthood, belongs also the offering of regular and special contributions to the Lord's work at home and abroad. Regarding this there is often evident among believers a widespread, very low, sometimes indeed, almost primitive standard of thinking and acting which is altogether unworthy of the kingdom of the Most High.

Offerings for church and mission work are not a mere matter of Christian charity. Missionaries, ministering brethren, preachers and pastors are not receivers of tips. If they had remained in their earthly callings, as scholars or scientists, factory owners or business men, engineers or officials, medical doctors or artists, office employees or artisans, many of them would have become most successful in their careers, and in many cases have earned a high income. It was the call from above which they willingly followed and thus devoted their whole life to the work of the Lord. How should the work of the gospel make progress in the world, if there were not, in every fresh generation, men and women who offer all their time and strength to the Lord who has called them? Plainly almost all foreign missionary work would be impossible, and many branches of gospel and church work at home also, such as colportage, tent missions, gospel campaigns. Of course, only such should become full-time workers who are also fully capable of fulfilling an earthly profession. Such as fail in an earthly calling are not likely to work fruitfully in the harvest-field of the Lord.

Offerings for church and mission work are, according to general New Testament conception, simply the *duty of the church* and all its members. It is not open to our choice whether or not we shall support the Lord's work at home and abroad. It is the *command* of the Risen Lord ("ordained": I Cor. 9: 14) and thus simply a question of practical obedience for every redeemed one. Offerings for the kingdom of God belong therefore to practical sanctification. By the manner of our actual submission to this Divine precept we can easily test ourselves as to how far we really and seriously recognize the Lordship of our Redeemer. Further:

Offerings for church and mission work are an *outward response for the spiritual blessing* we have received, a "communication with respect to giving and receiving" (Phil. 4: 15). Acknowledging a gift for missionary service from the Philippians, Paul wrote: "You have entered into a fellowship with me in the matter of giving and receiving" (see R.V.). This means that they gave the apostle bodily help and received through him spiritual blessings. To the Corinthians he writes: "If we sowed unto you spiritual things, is it a great matter if we shall reap your carnal [earthly] things?" (I Cor. 9: 7–11). Missionary gifts are an expression of our gratitude for the redemption we have received and for the service which Christ and His people have done and are doing in our souls. Christ claims this right, and all disobedience in this respect is contempt of His authority, it is even robbing God, according to the principle stated in Mal. 3: 7–10. It is, of course, true that offerings should not be given unwillingly but readily and with joy, "as each purposes in his heart" (II Cor. 9: 7). But if our hearts are full of thankfulness and love to Christ, all this will be done joyfully and in a way worthy of God. And more than this: In giving the giver is himself the receiver.

Offerings for church and mission work are *deposits in the bank of Heaven*, paid in by the giver himself and thus an everlasting advantage for his own blessing. As Paul puts it, it is "the profit which is entered to *your* credit," which increases in *your* account (Phil. 4: 17), which is credited as your "deposit" in the heavenly "savings bank." Each such paying out is in reality a paying in. "My God will give you according to His riches all that ye need in glorious fulness in Christ Jesus" (Phil. 4: 19; *cf.* Gal. 6: 6). And even still higher must this obligation of the saints be valued: it has a priestly character.

Offerings for the poor and for church and mission work are *New Testament sacrifices* and therefore a very important part of the practical realization of the general priesthood. If they are presented in the right attitude of heart, and correspondingly also in the right outward measure, they are "an odour of a sweet smell, a sacrifice acceptable, well-pleasing to God" (Phil. 4: 18). Thus Paul characterized the missionary gifts from the Philippians. You can test yourself as to how far you have really understood with your heart your standing and share in the general priesthood of the New Testament Church, by examining your own willingness to bring such practical, priestly sacrifices for the Lord's work and kingdom. By their attitude to money the true and false prophets of the Old Testament time could be distinguished (Micah 3: 11; Num. 22: 16). This was always regarded as an infallible criterion. Similarly, by the attitude to money also in the New Testament the genuineness and sincerity of all general priesthood can be tested. Finally:

Offerings for church and mission work are *a privilege and an honour* for the helper. "Make to yourselves friends by means of the mammon of unrighteousness; that, when it shall fail, they [the friends thus made] may receive you into the eternal tabernacles" (Luke 16: 9). How wonderful it will be when in eternity many connexions, hitherto often unknown, between victories on the mission-field and in the Lord's work in general will be made manifest! What a joy and what an honour it will be when we shall then perceive, and understand in the eternal light, how even our personal sacrifice had a share in the work of the Lord by helping to spread the Scriptures or by making possible some service through which souls were led to Christ. What happiness then to be privileged to see in all humility that while others fought and won the victory, yet I, by God's grace, was their fellow-combatant, although perhaps I was separated from the battle-field by thousands of miles. Such joy and honour can be the blessed result of the practical service and sacrifice of the New Testament general priesthood.

The real innermost centre of the New Testament general priesthood of the church and all its members, however, is the *life of prayer*. For the true New Testament priest, to pray is not a mere duty but a God-given privilege. Then the sins of others will be no more an object for unkind criticism but occasion and task for loving, intercessory prayer. The unholiness of others will be treated in a holy manner. It will not be carried into the "camp" but into the "sanctuary." From the quiet prayer chamber will go forth streams of blessing into church and home, into pastoral and evangelistic work (Eph. 6: 18, 19; Rom. 15: 30–32), yes, even into worldly governments and authorities and into the life of the nations (I Tim. 2: 1, 2).

Prayer is the "transformer," the "switching station," which passes on the "current" from God, the heavenly "power station," into the individual households, "workshops" and "plants" of everyday life, transforming it into life and power and passing it on to its various destinations. Without a life of prayer, no life of victory! Without taking, no having! Without living *in* Christ, no possibility of fruitfully working *for* Him! Even in the rush of our daily duties our communion with the Lord in prayer must never be interrupted.

But by itself praying is not all that is needed. Not all that is called prayer is *really* prayer. Even believers can "pray" unbelievingly. Their prayer can be a matter of form, it can be thoughtless, or even weakened by doubts, and "let not that man think that he shall receive anything of the Lord" (James 1: 7). Only prayer instinct with faith can help us, a real trustful waiting on the Lord to hear us in His good time and according to His counsel.

Such prayer is true priestly *work* for the Lord. It is not an activity of the soul which is merely additional to the other work of the priest, but it is the main part of the work itself, in fact, the most important work of all. In God's kingdom only he is a

abourer who is a man of prayer. For praying is working
(Col. 4: 12, 13). Only that local church is spiritually strong in
which the prayer-meetings are not the weak but the strong point
of the church life, and in which this regular prayer fellowship is a
real co-operation with the work of God at home and abroad.
The decisive battles in life are fought out in the prayer chamber.
As our prayer, so will be our work, and also our influence upon
our fellow-men. Prayer decides our whole attitude to all
problems of life. The quality of our work is dependent upon
the quality of our prayers. The priest of God must live in the
sanctuary.

In addition to prayers and supplications it is the special privilege of the priest to present before the Lord the offerings of
thanksgiving and worshipping.

Worship must be clearly distinguished from thanksgiving.
The latter is concerned with the *gifts* and the individual *blessings*
which God bestows upon His creatures, while the former is
concentrated upon the *Person* and *Nature* of the Giver
Himself.

Thanksgiving glorifies God for His *deeds* and demonstrations
of His glory. Worship, however, meditates upon and praises
the innermost secret and centre of this glory, that is the *Godhead*
Itself.

It is true that worship also speaks of the great facts of salvation and redemption; but in worship, in distinction to thanksgiving, we do not think so much of the *advantages* and *blessings*
for ourselves which arise out of these great facts and for which
we praise God, but rather we regard them as revelations and ever
new manifestations of the *inward nature* of the Divine Being.
Thanksgiving, thus, emphasizes the glorious *result* of the Divine
redemptive acts for the redeemed creature; worship praises
their Divine *foundation* and *source* in the heart of the Creator
Himself.

In thanksgiving our hearts rejoice over that which the Saviour
and Lord has accomplished for us *personally*; in worship our souls
rejoice in Him and praise Him, the holy God of all power and
love, for what He is in *Himself*.

Worship is, therefore, higher than thanksgiving, for worship
is freer from all things created and lives more in the eternal.
Worship looks away from all time, from the persons, things, and
events in its course, and to a certain degree even from the temporal revelations of the Godhead, and lifts itself up directly

to the heart of the Most High and there occupies itself with His own eternal, all-holy, all-loving Nature.

Therefore in the love-fellowship between Creator and creature worship is the summit of the responsive love of the creature. And inasmuch as man precisely in this his vocation as a creature had been called from the beginning to such a fellowship of love, he had therefore been called to worship and adoration of the great God. Worship is the first and most important object of man's eternal calling. From eternity to eternity the redeemed and glorified will be privileged to praise the Lord of Lords, saying exultantly: "Salvation to our God, who sitteth upon the throne, and unto the Lamb . . . Amen: Blessing, and glory, and wisdom, and thanksgiving, and honour, and power, and might, be unto our God for ever and ever, Amen" (Rev. 7: 10, 12). "But the hour cometh, and now is, when the true worshippers shall worship the Father in spirit and truth: for such doth the Father seek to be His worshippers. God is a Spirit: and they that worship Him must worship Him in spirit and truth" (John 4: 23, 24).

The service of a priest, however, should not be performed merely *in* the temple, but also effectively *outside*. He who is a "man of prayer" must also be a "man with a message."

Witnessing is therefore another essential part of the service of the New Testament general priesthood of the church and all its members, "For the priest's lips should keep knowledge, and they [the people] should seek the law at his mouth" (Mal. 2: 7). Let us take heed: Something is expected from us because we are priests of God! Often the world is quite unconscious of this their own expectation. Indeed, they would deny it most emphatically if they were told that they have such expectations. And yet it is true. And *we* are those who are responsible to give them the answer to their deepest and unsolved problems. For we are the only ones who *have* the answer. "This day is a day of good tidings, and we hold our peace: if we tarry . . . punishment will overtake us" (II Kings 7: 9). "I am debtor" (Rom. 1: 14). "Woe is unto me if I preach not the gospel" (I Cor. 9: 16). New Testament general priesthood and the proclamation of the gospel belong together. For this reason it is Paul's desire to "be a minister of Jesus Christ to the Gentiles, ministering the gospel of God, that the offering up of the Gentiles might be acceptable, being sanctified by the Holy Spirit" (Rom. 15: 16).

The original word used here for "ministering" (Gk. *hierour-gounta*) means literally "ministering in sacrifice" (R.V. mgn.), "ministering as about holy things," executing the office of a Christian priest, more spiritual, and therefore more excellent than the Levitical priesthood. Also the Greek word for "offering" (*prosphora*) which the apostle uses here, is an expression taken from priestly and temple service, meaning, the *oblation* of the Gentiles. "Long had the Jews been the holy nation, the kingdom of priests, but now the Gentiles are made priests unto God. Indeed, the Gentiles are themselves the sacrifice offered up to God by Paul, in the name of Christ, a living sacrifice, holy, acceptable to God" (Matthew Henry).

This whole passage in Romans shows how much Paul views as one the New Testament priesthood and the New Testament gospel and missionary activity. Indeed, mission work is, in the judgment of the great Apostle to the nations, an integral part of the practical realization of the New Testament general priesthood. To be a priest means to be a man with a mission, to be a witness for Christ, to be a co-worker in the spreading of the gospel at home and abroad.

Thus the church, being the New Testament priesthood, is at the same time Christ's prophet. It is the proclaimer and interpreter of His word of life to the world. It is witness and confessor, messenger and mouth of God, that is, a *missionary* church in its deepest inward nature. And let us bear in mind that the calling and obligation of the church is to be experienced and practised by all its individual members, not only in their collective co-operation, but also, indeed quite definitely, in each single personal life and service. Practical neglect of the missionary command of the Lord makes evident that the nature of the New Testament general priesthood has not been really understood, in fact, that the very character of the church itself has not been clearly conceived. For it belongs to the essence of the *ecclesia* that it is the church of the Word: It lives through the Word, it nourishes itself from the Word, it is strengthened by the Word, it orders its way according to the Word. Thus, in a certain sense, it should be also "word" itself, that is, message and mediator of the gospel by walk and witness, either by going oneself to the home or foreign mission-field or by supporting by prayer and practical fellowship those who have gone. The church of the Lord lives *through* mission work—for only by the carrying out of the missionary commission have other countries and homes been reached by the gospel. Therefore the church of the Lord and its individual members must also in practice live *for* mission work—the word "mission" being taken in its wide and original sense as witnessing, gospel preaching, winning souls at home and abroad. Thus we are ambassadors for Christ. Christ "speaks" through us "as though God did beseech . . . by us; we pray . . . in Christ's stead, be ye reconciled to God" (II Cor. 5: 20).

Again and again since the days of the Reformation the question has arisen as to the justification and possibility of missionary work. Many have answered in the negative, but the heroic pioneers of the gospel among many heathen nations have given an affirmative answer, with proof in word and deed, so impressive and irrefutable, that it cannot be overlooked. Men like Zinzendorf, Ziegenbalg, William Carey, Robert Morrison, David Livingstone, Hudson Taylor, those great banner-bearers of the good tidings of God's salvation in the wide world, have proved that missionary work is not only possible but, indeed, most urgently necessary.

In fact the missionary command of the Lord has never been withdrawn. On the contrary, it is inseparably bound up with the missionary promise: "And, lo, I am with you alway, even unto the consummation of the age." The missionary command and the missionary promise belong together. One cannot claim the one and practically deny the other. For if the *promise*: "I am with you always, even unto the consummation of the age" is still valid, then also the missionary *command*: "Go ye into all the world." In the parable of the pounds the Lord said to His servants: "Trade ye *till I come*" (Luke 19: 13). This means, do not cease beforehand! Be as men who, when the Lord comes, are found at work.

On the 4th of December, 1857, Livingstone, the great Africa explorer and missionary pioneer, visited the University of Cambridge. On this occasion he made an appeal to the students to devote themselves to the work of the Lord in Africa. Among other things he said: "I personally have never ceased to rejoice that God has entrusted me with this service. People talk a lot about the sacrifice involved in devoting my life to Africa. But can this be called a sacrifice at all if we give back to God a little of what we owe Him? And we owe Him so very much that we shall never be able to pay off our debt. Can that be called a sacrifice which gives to ourselves the deepest satisfaction, which develops our best powers, and justifies us in having the greatest hopes and expectations? Away with this word! Away with such thoughts! It is anything else than a sacrifice! Rather call it a *privilege*! For a moment fear, illness, sufferings, dangers, and the giving up of so many conveniences which seem to be indispensable for our life, may hold us back, but only for a moment. It is nothing to be compared with the glory which shall be revealed in us. I never offered a sacrifice!"

The Lord needs such servants, men and women in whose souls a holy fire is burning, who have only *one* main purpose for their life, that is, witnessing to and glorifying the Person of their Redeemer, making known His work of salvation by word and deed, spreading His kingly rule near and far. Such people are in truth priests unto God.

A hundred and sixty years ago, at the commencement of the new missionary era, during a discussion on India, a servant of the Lord said: "We see that there is a gold mine in India, and it is as deep as the centre of the earth, and who will there dare to explore it?" Then William Carey, who became later on the great missionary, linguist, Bible-translator, and pioneer of gospel work abroad, gave that classical answer: "I will go, I will descend this mine; but you must not forget firmly to hold the ropes!"

"Hold the ropes firmly!" Back up the witnesses of the gospel! Support them and pray for them! Be witnesses yourselves! "That ye stand fast in one spirit, with one soul striving for the faith of the gospel!" (Phil. 1: 27). Fellowship in God's kingdom means fellowship in God's work. Only so will fellowship in God's victory also be ultimately attained. This is the prophetic side of the calling of the New Testament general priesthood.

Let us therefore be on fire for this holy commission. Away with all indolence! Away with all powerless, self-centred, "pious," merely emotional looking on! We are not allowed to be simply passive onlookers of the actions and deeds of God. There is a dynamic power in the gospel to be spread over land and sea. We must not only make use of but even *seek* opportunities to bear witness for Christ and so bring others under the sound of the gospel. "Rescue the perishing, care for the dying, snatch them in pity from sin and the grave." The Son of God Himself came down to *seek* that which was lost. Do you *seek*? Do you rescue? Or do you think that an attitude of mere defence is sufficient to win the victory, so that no holy aggressiveness and initiative are required? In that case your Christian life and the practical realization of your share in the New Testament general priesthood have failed very much indeed!

> Only the wicked servant can stand still
> Looking on while his master storms the hill.

All want of missionary spirit is sickness of the soul. It belongs indispensably to a strong spiritual life to have the keen desire to win souls for Christ.

As the prophetic priesthood of God, the church of the Lord is the bearer of the most glorious message on earth. It is "the pillar and ground of the truth" (I Tim. 3: 15), the instrument for radiating the light of salvation, the representative of Christ as the true and faithful witness, and each individual is called to be a fellow-labourer in this priestly and prophetic commission of the whole church.

> Every priest of God — a witness!
> Every redeemed one — a missionary!
> Every local church — a church of workers!

To the building up of the church, however, the proclamation of the gospel and the experience of individual conversion are only the foundation, however indispensable and fundamental they are. The saved must be sanctified, their spiritual life must be deepened. The New Testament priests, as the bearers of the word of God, have therefore received another vital commission from the Lord. If the priest is the "messenger" of Jehovah and if the people seek the "law," *i.e.*, the Word of God, "at his mouth" (Mal. 2: 7), then he will have to administer not only the evangelistic, but also the pastoral word of God, and will thus have to perform also the personal work of the *shepherd* of souls. Therefore pastoral work is another most important responsibility of the New Testament general priesthood.

Priestly souls are shepherds in the church. They have an eye for the distresses and needs of others. Their eyes have been opened. They do not view their surroundings with the sharp look of unloving criticism but with hearts full of love, graciousness, and compassion. They endeavour to see the good side in the character of others, their upright intentions and sincere strivings and efforts, and to have these in mind as points of contact in their spiritual approach. In the sanctuary of God they receive the word of wisdom to help others and lead them on,

K

practically and spiritually. They see, of course, the imperfections of these others; but at the same time, like their heavenly High Priest, they have sympathy with their weaknesses (Heb. 4: 15). In all this they are perfectly aware of their own imperfections, for the Spirit of God causes them to know their own heart, thus making them humble and gracious.

They do not generalize everything but understand each separate situation in its own special character. Their relationships to others are not cold and stiff, not merely objective, but warm-hearted and kind to everyone. The spiritual welfare of each individual lies upon their hearts. They have intuition and can understand even those characters which may be very different from their own disposition of soul. In conversation they practise the high and noble art of listening to others.

They free themselves from their own aspects of things, their own circle of interests, their own self-centred forms of expression, their own prejudiced view-points, their own ideas and criteria. They endeavour to take a stand outside at a certain distance from themselves in order to overcome the distance which separates them from others. They step out of their own Ego and place themselves in the position of those they desire to help.

Thus the true priestly, personal worker leaves behind his own "Self," meets the personality of the one he is dealing with, and thus can attain real fellowship with him. He recognizes the standard and view-point of the other man. Here they start, walking on together, and at last reach the higher ideals and aims, now common to them both.

Of vital importance in priestly personal work is the right way to give spiritual admonishment and encouragement. There are four kinds of admonition:

The hard-hearted admonition. This is the merciless lecture which, without feeling, points out rudely the mistakes and failings of the other, humbles and belabours him, condemns and judges him in a high-handed manner. The only result of such kind of admonition is the creating in the heart of the other a new front-line of resistance which perhaps had not before existed. Such "workers" are always standing before closed doors. They have themselves shut the doors of other hearts. They make them hard-hearted and stubborn, bitter and burdened. They are not priests at all, but Pharisees. They do not bear the burdens of souls, but are themselves a burden to such souls.

Against this very type of degenerated "shepherding" Jesus fought in the Sermon on the Mount, saying: "Why beholdest thou the mote that is in thy brother's eye, but considerest not the beam that is in thine own eye? Or how wilt thou say to thy brother, Let me cast out the mote out of thine eye; And, lo a beam is in thine own eye? Thou hypocrite, cast out first the beam out of thine own eye; and then shalt thou see clearly to cast out the mote out of thy brother's eye" (Matt. 7: 3-5).

The second kind is:

The legal admonition. This commands and gives orders. It makes use of the categorical "Thou shalt." It appeals to "the goodwill," the sense of honour and self-respect of the other person. It approaches the moral character of man. The result is at best that good resolutions are taken, a new attempt at moral reform, a new stirring up of all inner energy. The final result is, however, always and only—*defeat.* For by the law cometh only "knowledge" of, but no victory over, sin (Rom. 3: 20; 8: 3). This latter is accomplished only by grace. Yet this legal admonition stands on a much higher level than the hard-hearted type, which in reality is no admonition at all.

The third kind is:

The reasonable admonition. This rises still higher than the legal type. Therefore it is also more fruitful. Of course, the legal type of admonition should not be completely rejected. Although it is not able to attain the full, spiritual aim, it has, in the general history of salvation (*cf.* Mosaic Law), as well as in all individual education, a God-given place. The father commands his little son even when it is not possible to explain to him the reason for so doing. The son has to obey simply because his father has given the order, and he is right if he does so, even if he is not able to understand his father's reasons.

Reasonable admonition, however, reaches deeper into the inner life of the one being admonished. It makes clear *why* something is ordered. It not only commands but convinces. It makes the command understandable. The one addressed is treated with more respect in that he is not required to render mere outward obedience, but at the same time is enabled to understand inwardly. This raises his own personality and makes him happier and more willing. His obedience comes more from his heart and is therefore nobler.

But the fourth kind of admonition alone can attain the God-intended end:

The creative, spiritual admonition. This includes indeed both commanding and explaining, but goes further than these in that the working power of the Holy Spirit is present and is, indeed, the real, essential, decisive factor. This leads to a clear view of the situation and to conviction, to a loosening of bondage and a real inner deliverance, to Spirit-wrought "purpose of heart" and genuine decision of the will (Acts 11: 23). It leads to purification and, if necessary, compensation, to increased devotion and full surrender to the Lord. After repenting and humbling oneself, new courage will be found. Not only forgiveness but practical sanctification will be the result. Not only a new thinking but a new acting will be the fruit. And with strong courage and confidence we shall go on our way rejoicing.

Thus creative admonition always includes encouragement. In the language of the New Testament, "admonition" and "encouragement" are indeed the same Greek word (*paraklesis*, verb *parakaleo*). He who does not know how to encourage has no spiritual right to admonish. Admonition without encouragement is in most cases nothing but depressing criticism. To a fruitful admonition belongs a confident attitude of mind, directing the other to the ever-renewing powers of the Holy Spirit. Only thus, in the love and with the heart of Jesus Christ (Phil. 1: 8), will the New Testament priest of God be able to carry out the fruitful work of shepherding. For Spirit-filled love is the heart and soul of all true personal work. He who does not love, cannot serve. He is simply unable to "find" the other one. He gets no inner contact with him. Only the love of the Holy Spirit, and happy confidence in His power and His working in the soul of the other, render us capable of carrying out fruitfully the commission for pastoral work as an integral part of the New Testament general priesthood.

All this makes the New Testament general priesthood a channel of blessing. To be a blessing means to bring others into contact with God, to lay the name of Jehovah upon them. "On this wise ye shall bless the children of Israel; ye shall say unto them, The Lord [Jehovah] bless thee and keep thee: the Lord [Jehovah] make His face to shine upon thee, and be gracious unto thee: the Lord [Jehovah] lift up His countenance upon thee, and give thee peace. So shall they [the priests] put (lay) My name upon the children of Israel; and I will bless them" (Num. 6: 23–27).

But he who is not willing to partake in the service of practical *sacrifice* has no right to talk about the general priesthood of the church.   He who is not prepared to fulfil the expectations of the world and be a co-worker in the *spread of the word* and testimony of God by offering missionary gifts, missionary prayer, by devotion of his spare time, and by personal witness for Christ, has no right to talk of the priesthood of all believers, for his talk is empty.   It is without life and reality.   Let not that man say that he really believes in the general priesthood of the church who does not lead a life of *prayer* and does not take regular part in the spiritual warfare of prayer in the church gatherings.   If we speak unkindly about others, instead of praying for them or helping them by *personal work and shepherding*, we must realize that we thereby deny in practice our part in the general priesthood of the church.

Being a "priest" does not only mean having a privileged spiritual position, but being entrusted with a God-given commission, not only having received an honour, but a holy order. It is not only that we possess a name of dignity but that we lead at the same time a life of practical service.   Whether a person has really understood the meaning and importance of the general true priesthood of all believers can in many ways be more discerned outside than inside the church building, chapel, or meeting-hall. Thus here also the word is true: "These ought ye to have done, and not to leave the other undone" (Matt. 23: 23).   In all this the special emphasis lies on standing the test in the practice of our everyday life.   Furthermore:

General priesthood and the local church.   Just as the individual believer, so also the Christian local church should practically take part in the New Testament general priesthood.   Also here we must learn to think and act again on more Biblical and New Testament lines.   A local church which is not missionary-minded must either repent or it will one day have to retreat. Either we "appear" as Christ's witnesses or we shall have to "disappear."   The Lord places before everyone this alternative: Either we do "mission" work or the ultimate result will be our "demission."   Either we keep "on the move" or be "removed!"   Either we shine, or the lampstand of the local church will be taken away from its place (Rev. 2: 5).   The branch which does not bear fruit will be cut off (John 15: 6). According to the clear order revealed in the Scriptures the priest is a "messenger of God" (Mal. 2: 7).   He who will not be God's witness and messenger denies practically his share in the general priesthood. This is true both with regard to the individual as well as to the local church.

A local church which is not actually connected with the work of the proclamation of the gospel, either by prayer or by sending out home workers or foreign missionaries or by contributing regular gifts to the mission-field is either sick or spiritually undeveloped. Laziness in witnessing and lameness in missionary zeal is a practical ignoring of the world-embracing significance of Christ's priestly sacrifice on Golgotha.

Mission work is a divine "must." "Remission of sins should (*must*) be preached in His name among all nations, beginning at Jerusalem" (Luke 24: 47). It is not left to our own choice whether or not we will testify to the world the message of the cross. The command of the glorified Christ is in the background. The true Christian confesses with Jeremiah: "Jehovah, Thou hast persuaded me and I was persuaded; Thou art stronger than I, and hast prevailed" (Jer. 20: 7).[1] He declares with Peter: "For we cannot but speak the things which we saw and heard (Acts 4: 20). He confesses with Paul: "For necessity is laid upon me" (I Cor. 9: 16).

As a "priesthood" the church and its individual members have the commission to "proclaim." "But ye are an elect race, a royal *priesthood*, a holy nation . . . that ye may *show forth* the praises [virtues, excellencies] of Him who called you out of darkness into His marvellous light" (Gk. *exangeilēte, proclaim aloud* by word and action, I Pet. 2: 9).

Local churches, according to the New Testament, are not places for preserving and conserving Christian teaching and truth. They are not to be pious, self-centred circles for emotional "self-edification," but rather places where a real, spiritual "building-up" takes place. And let everyone take care *how* he builds (I Cor. 3: 10). It is not enough simply to hold *fast* the truth but to hold it *up*, like a standard, a flag of victory carried ahead of the warriors of Christ's army. One cannot separate in practice the New Testament calling to be a "priest" from the calling to be a "proclaimer," a mouth of God, a "prophet." Priestly souls are

---

[1] The Authorized Version reads: "O Lord, thou hast deceived me, and I was deceived." To this we remark: The word "deceived" (A.V.), "enticed" (R.V. footnote) may be very well translated "persuaded". Matthew Henry in his Commentary points to the fact that in this sense the word is used in Gen. 9: 27 margin: "God shall persuade Japhet." And Prov. 25: 15: "By much forbearance is a prince persuaded." And Hos. 2: 14: "I will allure (persuade) her."

soul-winners. God's temple is a bright life-centre, radiating eternal light (*cf.* Rev. 21: 24).

In this respect the prayer gatherings of believers have a special significance. Church prayer and world-wide mission work belong inseparably together. If ever the inward oneness of the prophetic-missionary commission and the general priesthood of the church is evident, it is manifest here. In a sound local church the priestly prayer for the prophetic proclamation of God's gospel must occupy a large space. Every prayer meeting in the local church should be a time of united practical striving for and co-operation with God's servants on the mission-field at home and abroad (Rom. 15: 30–32; Col. 4: 3–4; Eph. 6: 18–20).

This will become at the same time a source of reviving and blessing for the local church itself. In such practising of the New Testament general priesthood the local church experiences something of the universality, the super-national, spiritual unity of the whole church of God.

It will help to stir up and stimulate the prayer meetings if reports from the mission-field and personal letters from missionaries are publicly read to the gathering. Thus the prayers will become more concrete, the requests more manifold, and everything will be more direct, more personal, filled with more life and spirit.

Therefore: Only such a local church is fully realizing its share in the New Testament general priesthood which is

a local church with Spirit-filled, regularly well-attended prayer meetings;

a local church with members who are practical helpers and fellow-workers with the Lord's servants in the world-wide harvest-field;

a local church with persevering, energetic activity in the preaching of the gospel, by tract distribution, personal witness, and, wherever possible, open-air meetings;

a local church with a warm-hearted, spiritual atmosphere of love, where everyone tries to help the other by mutual care and charity in a prayerful spirit, considering one another to provoke unto love and good works.

In such a local church the gatherings and services also will be under the guidance of the Holy Spirit, and the gifts of the Holy Spirit, as distributed by the Lord Himself, will be developed in their God-appointed variety, in brotherly fellowship, in dependence upon Christ, and thus in holy freedom of the Spirit (I Cor. 12: 4–11; 14: 26). And when the church is gathered together at the Lord's Table praising the priestly sacrifice on Golgotha, priestly worship will rise up to the heavenly Sanctuary, thus crowning the privilege of the general priesthood of the church.

3. *The kingdom of the church.* The Scripture links the priesthood with the kingdom, the heavenly throne with the heavenly temple (comp. Isa. 6: 1–4). Therefore also the church is not only a priestly people but at the same time a kingdom (Rev. 1: 6; I Pet. 2: 9), indeed, it is a "kingdom of priests" (*cf.* Ex. 19: 6). This present and future royal dignity is the third great possession contained in the birthright of the church of the firstborn. As such the church will one day be the "Imperial Staff" of the heavenly King, "the ruling aristocracy" in the coming kingdom of God. "Fear not, little flock; for it is your Father's good pleasure to give you the kingdom" (Luke 12: 32). "Know ye not that the saints shall judge the world?" (I Cor. 6: 2). The redeemed will one day even rule over angels: "Know ye not that we shall judge angels?" (I Cor. 6: 3). "He that overcometh I will give to him to sit down with Me in My throne, as I also overcame, and sat down with My Father in His throne" (Rev. 3: 21). "The Lord God giveth them light: and they shall reign for ever and ever" (Rev. 22: 5).

III. THE SERIOUS DANGER

But the writer to the Hebrews does not really speak about the birthright of Esau in order to show the glories of the church but in order to give a warning. Especially when considered against the background of such high dignities, failure in Christian life is all the more deplorable and reprehensible. We must see the dangers and behave ourselves accordingly. We must count the cost not only of faithful Christian discipleship, as the Lord says (Luke 14: 28), but also what it means to be *un*faithful! For the "reward" of such sin would be nothing less than the loss of the enjoyment of most important privileges contained in the full possession of the birthright.

Doubtless, birthright is not identical with sonship. Esau remained Isaac's son even after he had rejected his birthright. In fact, he received, in spite of his great failure, a kind of secondary blessing (Gen. 27: 38, 40b). "By faith Isaac *blessed* Jacob *and* Esau concerning things to come" (Heb. 11: 20). But nevertheless he suffered an immense loss.

A similar experience, in a spiritual sense, can be the result of unfaithfulness for the New Testament "firstborn." Their life-relationship with the heavenly Father remains and will never be dissolved; for they have passed out of death into life (I John 3: 14). But very great heavenly values are at stake.

Possession of special heavenly riches, position as priests, and the royal dignity of ruling are the three God-appointed honours contained in the birthright. But:

In spite of all *riches* we may live in spiritual poverty. No overflowing of heavenly fulness may be evident. No inward richness may shine out. No joy of happy redemption may be manifest. Although children of eternal joy, we may walk about sorrowful and depressed, and instead of having our enjoyment and delight in our blessed Lord, we may look back full of longing to the empty joys and goods of this world.

In spite of our *priestly position* we may live no priestly prayer life! There may be no priestly heart and mind! No loving supplication! No witness as God's priestly messenger to the world! No happy gratefulness for so many rich blessings received! No genuine priestly worshipping of God in spirit and in truth! And finally:

In spite of our high *kingly calling* we may live practically like slaves. All earthly-mindedness is slavery. It is a denial of our heavenly nobility (Col. 3: 1–3). All sinful striving for money or earthly goods makes the "king" to be a "beggar." All worrying is unkingly. All fear of man is unworthy of a child of the great Heavenly Father and Sovereign. All over-sensitiveness and so easily feeling hurt and offended is small-mindedness. It is piteous and primitive. In fact, all service of sin makes him who is appointed to be a ruler to become practically a degraded servant, and sin which is in reality defeated behaves itself as if it were the victor and therefore acts as regent and tyrant, when in truth the Christian should be the overcomer.

Thus the believer, although belonging to the church of the firstborn, may practically deny his birthright. Instead of riches inward poverty, instead of priesthood practical separation from God, instead of kingship actual slavery!

How grave will be the consequences for eternity! Though indeed personally saved, yet how great the loss! Even Paul, the apostle of free grace, expressly emphasizes that the day of Christ will be revealed for the church "in fire." "The fire shall try every man's work of what sort it is" (I Cor. 3: 13). Thus it may happen that the life-work of a believer—possibly even yours!— will be burnt up, even though you yourself are saved, yet so as through fire, *i.e.*, like a brand plucked out of the burning, "as one who in a fire could only save his bare life" (I Cor. 3: 15). The position of being a child of God is, indeed, not forfeitable, but not the total fulness of the heavenly birthright. In this sense there is urgent need to give diligence to make our calling and election sure. "For thus shall be richly supplied unto you the entrance into the eternal kingdom of our Lord and Saviour Jesus Christ" (II Pet. 1: 10, 11).

IV. THE GRAVE ERROR

What was the fatal error into which Esau fell and which in this letter is held up to us as a warning? He sold his birthright for one mess of pottage. One can actually feel his uncontrolled greediness and gluttony in his words: "Let me eat of that red pottage, of that red pottage." In the original Hebrew text the words "of that red pottage" occur not only once but twice, so as to picture his greediness and want of self-control. Also his materialistic outlook and egoism sounds from his words: "I am at the point to die . . . what profit shall the birthright do to me?" (Gen. 25: 30–32).

From all this we see:

Esau lived for things visible and bartered for them things spiritual, *i.e.*, the only true values, the things which are real.

Esau lived for human enjoyment and bartered away God-given blessings.

Esau lived without discipline and self-control and bartered away his position of authority and honour.

Esau "despised" God's promise and offer of dignity and brought himself thereby into shame (Gen. 27: 37).

He lived for his own Ego and thus bartered away the high calling of his family.

He lived for the present and bartered away his noble commission for the future.

He lived for the fleeting moment and bartered for it eternal treasures.

Through all this he proved himself to be a godless and profane man. He was a secularized son of an elect patriarch, that is, he was a worldly-minded descendant of a God-devoted bearer of high Divine promises. He esteemed a passing enjoyment above most noble permanent privileges ordained of God. He "despised" his birthright (Gen. 25: 34). The Hebrew text uses a vigorous word here. The Septuagint, the Greek translation of the Old Testament, uses the word *phaulizo* which means that Esau regarded the birthright as a mere paltry thing and so gave it away for a trifle. In all this the profanity of Esau's heart and mind is shown.

For this reason God, who on account of His super-temporality, can already see everything before it actually begins, declared even before the birth of the two brothers: "Jacob have I loved but Esau have I hated" (Mal. 1: 2, 3; Rom. 9: 13). This does not mean a hostile animosity and hatred but refusal and rejection.

But for this sin and failure of Esau the birthright would have remained *his* privilege, and all successive developments in the whole history of salvation, right up to Christ the Messiah, would have used *him* and *his* descendants as channel and human instrument. Or, expressed more negatively, the whole further realization of the Divine redemptive plans would have taken its course *via* Esau and his family and *not via* Jacob ("Israel").

But now we see him weeping and lamenting and begging for the blessing (Gen. 27: 34). But he could not alter Isaac's attitude. Isaac had spoken as a prophet of God under the inspiration of the Spirit, and his God-inspired prophetic utterance could not be recalled. Esau "found no place for a change of mind in his father" (*American Standard Version*). There was "no room" to cancel his father's decision. The backslider is always the great loser.

This appears to be the sense of the words: He found no room for the "altering of mind" although he tried with tears. The Greek word *metanoia*, which otherwise means in the Scripture "repentance," can in this place hardly have this sense. For if anyone seeks "repentance" with tears he *is* already repentant and cannot be spoken of as not being able to find room for repentance. His many tears would indeed prove that he was repentant, *i.e.*, that he *had* altered his mind. For this reason most modern interpreters take the word *metanoia*, "altering," either as referring to Isaac in the sense that Isaac was begged by Esau to change his mind regarding his decision to take away the birthright from Esau and transfer it to Jacob (thus *e.g.*, Zwingli), *or*, since in the Greek text there is no reference at all to the person of Isaac, they take the word "*metanoia*" (= altering) in the sense of changing a situation, cancelling an order. In this sense of "cancellation" the Greek word *metanoia* is in fact often used in other Greek texts, for instance, papyri. Esau found no room for cancelling the transference of the blessing from him to Jacob, although he tried with tears. This also agrees with the Old Testament account, which never refers to Esau as having sought an inward change of heart with many tears. On the contrary, the Old Testament history shows quite clearly that he sought the outward blessing (Gen. 27: 34, 38).

This is also proved by his word in Gen. 27: 36 which he said of his brother: "Is he not rightly named Jacob [One that takes by the heel; Supplanter. Gen. 25: 26]? For he hath supplanted me these two times: he took away my birthright; and, behold, now he hath taken away my blessing." Thus he was blaming Jacob, not reproaching himself. "He mourned his loss but not his sin. In this also he proved himself a true son of his first parents, for Eve and Adam each blamed another for their guilty conduct. In each of the three cases there was a measure of truth, for those others blamed were in part responsible; but godly sorrow for sin seeks no such shelter, but accepts its own responsibility and is humble. This change of mind Esau neither showed nor sought" (G. H. Lang).

And what did he receive in exchange for the birthright? A mess of pottage!

Thus miserably does sin pay her servants!

My reader, read the above sentences again and ask yourself if they may not be a reflection of your own spiritual and practical attitude, even if perhaps not always, yet possibly often enough. Therefore take heed to the warning of this passage in *Hebrews!* So much hangs in the balance: glorious eternal gain or irretrievable loss.

In that disastrous moment Esau, at the cost of the future, had chosen satisfaction for the present. The mess of pottage pleased him for the moment. But finally the great disappointment came.

Thus he experienced in his own life the principle of the word of the Lord: "He that loveth his life shall lose it" (John 12: 25). "For what is a man profited, if he shall gain the whole world, and lose (damage) his own life?" (Matt. 16: 26).

The warrior of faith must act in just the opposite way. This is testified also by Paul. The Pauline epistles and the letter to the Hebrews show many similarities in thought and sometimes also of expression. Just as Paul, in various places in his epistles, uses the picture of the racecourse in the arena of faith so also the Writer of Hebrews does here at the very beginning of this our chapter. It is in the light of these opening words on the race and the joy which is set before the runner, that the reference of this our same chapter to the "birthright" ought to be read. Both are great possibilities; but both are forfeitable as regards the fulness of their eternal possession and enjoyment. Therefore the unreserved devotion of all our life and spiritual energy is needed in order to attain the full prize, the "crown," the "joy that is set before us" (cf. Heb. 12: 2), the "birthright" in its God-appointed, all-embracing, threefold totality as special abundance of riches, heavenly priesthood, glorified kingship.

Thus also Paul says: "And if also a man contend in the games, yet he is not crowned, except he have contended lawfully" (II Tim. 2, 5).

What does it mean "to contend lawfully," i.e., according to the rules of the athletic games? He transgresses the rules of the games who tries by some trick or other to win an easy victory. For instance, he may attempt to shorten the length of his racecourse by cutting corners. Thus he may seek to make his task easier than it really is. By this means in the earthly athletic games he may indeed reach the goal earlier than the others, but the umpire will not recognize such a "victory." In the same way, many today who desire to be real Christians, seek to avoid the heat of the battle by making certain compromises here and there. Of course, they too want to reach the goal, but they think it can be reached by paying a lower price. Let us not be deceived in this matter! Christ the Lord expects our whole devotion. Away with all compromises! Away with all attempts to make the narrow way somewhat broader and more passable! The Lord seeks our whole heart. Otherwise He cannot use our service and will not crown our efforts. In order to win the eternal crown we must offer our whole life.

In Rome, in the centre of the Piazza del Popolo, one of the busiest places of the city, I saw an ancient, very impressive Egyptian obelisk, 30 yards high. It was formerly in the Circus Maximus, that huge and magnificent sports stadium of the Roman Empire, the beginnings of which can be traced back to before the foundation of the Roman Republic (King Tarquinius Priscus, 500 B.C.). From the midst of the ruins of that ancient circus Pope Sixtus V 400 years ago caused this obelisk to be brought and erected on its present site. It is one of the oldest monuments which Rome possesses. The ancient Egyptian hieroglyphic inscription upon it, which can still be read today, indicates that it was originally set up in the time of the great Pharaoh Rameses II in the ancient town of Heliopolis,[1] a special centre of Egyptian sun-worship, between the thirteenth and twelfth centuries B.C., and thus from two hundred to three hundred years before David and Solomon. The Emperor Augustus had it brought from Egypt to Rome in the year 10 B.C., and set it up in the huge Circus Maximus in order to honour the sun-god Apollo. Placed in the "Spina," that is, the "barrier" in the middle of the arena which was ornamented with many statues, it formed, so to speak, the central point of this huge sports stadium.

From the Palatine, the place of the Imperial palaces, near the Forum Romanum, the Market Place of ancient Rome, standing not far from the ruins of the palace of the Emperor Augustus, I saw over the widespread ruins of this largest sports stadium of the ancient world. No less than 200,000 spectators could be seated there.

This ancient Egyptian sun-obelisk was the point which all partakers in the chariot and other races had to pass round. It made it impossible to cut any curve in the course. Each and every competitor in the races, be he chariot driver or runner, had to cover the full length of the course. No one could shorten the race for himself. No one could make the victory easier by any measure of his own. Each had to devote all his strength and to take upon himself the whole task without any abatement. Only thus was there any prospect of winning the prize.

For all those who know its history, this ancient Egyptian obelisk is even today an eloquent witness to all this.

Let us not be deceived! There is no victory without zeal and devotion, no complete triumph without giving up our own indolence, no real "Yes" to God without a practical "No" to self, sin, and the world! If any bad habit or sin should have a hold upon you, or if there should be any guilt of the past which has not yet been put right, put these things in order, clear them away in the power of the Lord, even if it should be hard to do so. If there exists any tension between yourself and another, if there is any possibility, seek to have a personal talk with the one

---

[1] Heliopolis, not far from modern Cairo (Egyptian On, Hebrew Beth-Schemesh, Jer. 43: 13), was at the time of the patriarchs the home city of Joseph's father-in-law, Potiphera. The latter was priest of the sun-god Ra (Gen. 41: 45; 46: 20).

concerned, even if it mean that you must humble yourself. And do it today. Do not postpone it to some later date. It might happen that then it will be postponed again, and in the end nothing will be done at all. Whenever the Lord entrusts you with a service of love and charity, do it with all your might, even if it should involve a sacrifice of time or money. If there is opportunity of witnessing to Christ, open your mouth joyfully, even if you are mocked at or have to suffer loss or disadvantage in your earthly career.

All this certainly costs self-denial. But self-denial is indispensable (Matt. 16: 24, 25). Every attempt to make the fight easier, makes the real victory more difficult and doubtful. Unless we submit ourselves to all Divine orders, and take up our full responsibility, we shall never attain the radiant and glorious prize on the coronation day.

V. The Hour of Decision

In Esau's bitter experience we can see something of the tactics used by sin. Sin uses the "weak moments" in the life of a man to cause his fall. Esau was "tired" when he made his fatal wrong decision (Gen. 25: 29). "Feed me, I pray thee, with that same red pottage; for I am faint (tired)" (v. 30).

This is the regular method of sin. Sin knows the weak points and critical moments of our life and is ever ready like a wild beast to jump upon its prey.

Thus Cain had his weak moment when jealousy took hold of him and he murdered his brother (Gen. 4: 5–8).

David had his weak moment and fell deep into sin, which then brought him and the house of Uriah into so much misery (II Sam. 11: 2–5; 17: 26ff.).

Peter had his weak moment when he denied his Master at the camp fire before a servant girl (Mark 14: 66–72).

Ananias and Sapphira had their weak moment when they behaved as hypocrites with regard to their offering for the Lord's work, and for this sin they were blotted out of the church and of life (Acts 5: 1–10).

But just these weak moments are the hours of decision. At such occasions it becomes clear what sort of persons we really are. The strength of a chain lies in the weakest link. A battlefront is broken through when the thinnest part of the line is pierced.

For this reason defeats in weak moments can never be excused by pointing to the unfavourable or unexpected circumstances. Not the march past in the review, but the battle shows the real quality of a soldier. We are only that which we prove to be in difficult conditions. The weak moments are the "examinations" and "tests" in our life of faith. The circumstances are only the battle*field*, they are never the actual decisive factors in the battle itself.

The first men sinned in Paradise. They fell into sin in surroundings which offered the most favourable conditions for a life according to God's will. On the other hand we read of the church in Pergamum: "I know . . . where thou dwellest, even where Satan's throne is: and thou holdest fast My name, and didst not deny My faith . . . where Satan dwelleth" (Rev. 2: 13). Let us note that in this word of the Lord the expression "where Satan dwelleth" occurs twice. In Pergamum all the circumstances were *against* the Christians and yet they remained faithful witnesses. Thus one can lose Paradise in Paradise, but one can confess the name of Christ even where Satan has his throne. The condition of the spiritual life *in* us is never dependent upon the circumstances *around* us, but only on our relationship to the heavenly world *above* us, and to the throne of God as its centre and to Him who sits upon the throne. This is of the highest importance as regards all superficial attempts at self-excuse, because it takes away from us every possibility of thinking and asserting that, when we fall into sin, it is our difficult circumstances and not we ourselves that are responsible for the defeat. And yet it is most encouraging, because now we know that no conditions *around* us are able to pluck us by force out of our fellowship with our Lord and Saviour, the great God *above* us. "For I am persuaded, that neither death, nor life, nor angels, nor principalities, nor things present, nor things to come, nor powers, nor height, nor depth, nor any other creation shall be able to separate us from the love of God, which is in Christ Jesus our Lord" (Rom. 8: 38, 39).

The same is true with regard to our service as witnesses. How many a believer excuses his failure in witnessing by pointing to the unfavourable surroundings. He is silent where he should speak, and some may have even given up entirely to testify to Christ, excusing themselves by referring to the "hard soil" which would in any case render their testimony unfruitful. Thus not seldom God-given opportunities are missed, and possibilities for powerful victory become "weak moments" full of defeat.

And yet, testifying is possible everywhere. There never was a time during which the world was without God's witnesses (Heb. 11) and there never will be.

In fact, very often just such times, when many adversaries are fighting against God's work, are special seasons of "open doors." Paul, the great pioneer missionary among the apostles, says: "a great door and effectual is opened unto me, and there are many adversaries" (I Cor. 16: 9). Open doors and adversaries very often belong one to another. Special hatred against the message of the gospel and special opportunities for victorious witnessing to Christ have often appeared together in the history of the church. Only we must learn again to be better witnesses. God has no need of defenders and advocates, nor of experts and masters of rhetoric, but what He desires are wholly devoted men and women who know only one theme and who have only one passion, that is, Himself, the great God, Jesus Christ (II Cor. 4: 5). Personal witness from man to man was the evangelizing method practised by the early church. In this respect, too, we must become again "early Christians," and then we shall experience that the work of the Lord always shares and repeats the history of its Divine Master: opposed by the world, yet not defeated; rejected by unbelief, yet not refuted; given over to death by men, yet always full of resurrection life; dead, buried and yet always rising again. "The voice of rejoicing and salvation is in the tents of the righteous" (Psa. 118: 15).

If this is our attitude, God-given opportunities for witness will not become "weak moments" in our life but occasions to save souls and thus times of triumphant joy in heaven and earth (Luke 15: 7).

VI. The Birthright and the Heavenly Prize

The warning reference to Esau and to the loss of his birthright is given in Hebrews 12 in connexion with a message which begins by demanding of us that we should run in the arena of faith. "Let us run with patience the race that is set before us" (Heb. 12: 1). It is a message which demands of us a purposeful perseverance in the running of the course (v. 1), an overcoming of all signs of fatigue and all symptoms of weakness (vv. 3–12), a pressing on in Spirit-wrought energy. "Therefore lift up the

L

hands which hang down and the feeble knees" (v. 12). "Make straight paths for your feet" (v. 13). "Follow after! Pursue . . .!" (v. 14).

In this connexion God's Word expressly emphasizes great dangers that are imminent in case the fighter is failing in the battle. Instead of running in the race you may "be turned out of the way by lameness" (v. 13). Instead of living in spiritua-fulness, you may "fall short of the grace of God" (v. 15). Inl stead of being a channel of blessing for others you may be a poisonous plant defiling many (v. 15). And the Spirit of God would arouse us with the alarming exhortation: "Follow after [pursue] peace with all men, and the sanctification *without which no man shall see the Lord!*" (v. 14). For the prize will not be given for nothing, but demands the energy of faith and practical faith-fulness. In view of the context of our chapter the prize of the race is regarded as the full enjoyment of the heavenly birthright.

Five main facts show us the nature of the prize.

The heavenly prize is not to be expected as a matter of course but must be earnestly contended for. Justification is a gift of free grace, but the measure of glorification depends upon personal devotion and steadfastness in the race. Thus it may happen that a believer does not stand the test, and the Umpire of the races, "the Lord, the righteous judge" (II Tim. 4: 8), will declare him "disquali-fied" at the prize-giving (I Cor. 9: 27). He receives no crown of victory. "That I myself might not be rejected after having preached to others." The word "rejected" used in the original text (Gk. *adokimos*) is the technical term for a runner not standing the test before the master of the games and therefore being ex-cluded at the prize-giving. This is a possibility to be taken very seriously by every believer. And yet:

The heavenly prize is not identical with eternal salvation but is asso-ciated with various degrees of glorification. In spite of the grave possibility of being "disqualified" at the end, the runner who did not hold out in the race will not be eternally lost. Even in the case of Esau, in spite of his loss of the birthright, there remained the relationship of son. Although, indeed, Holy Scripture speaks in very strong terms of suffering "loss" (I Cor. 3: 15), of "being ashamed" at Christ's coming (I John 2: 28), of one's whole life-work being "burned up" (I Cor. 3: 13, 15b) so that one is saved "yet so as through fire"; yet it clearly testifies the fact that also such an one *will be* "saved."

Thus grace and reward are presented as combined with one

another and yet shown as harmonious opposites, just like the poles of a magnetic needle are opposites and yet belong together inseparably. And thus being saved and being glorified, being born again and being perfected, receiving grace and becoming a receiver of the crown, that is, the entering into the arena at the beginning and the prize-giving at the end, stand before our eyes in their mutual relationship.

Through all this the twofold result in our daily life should be joy and earnestness, thankfulness and sense of responsibility, certainty of salvation and fear of God. Only in the realization of these two opposite and harmonious poles in Christian experience, is true Biblical sanctification possible.

The heavenly prize is not equal for each, but will be graduated according to faithfulness. The three main blessings of the New Testament birthright are heavenly riches, priestly service, and royal dignity, and full possession of this birthright is the prize.

The more a member of the "church of the firstborn" has made a fruitful use of the spiritual *riches* intrusted to him by the Lord during his life-time, the more he will enjoy the fulness of blessing in eternity (*cf.* Matt. 25: 21, 23).

The more a member of the "church of the firstborn" has actually realized the rights and obligations of the general *priesthood*, the greater and more glorious will be his service as priest in the heavenly temple (Rev. 3: 12; I Pet. 1: 5, 4).

The more a member of the "church of the firstborn" has lived worthily of his high *royal calling* here on earth, the higher will be his position in the kingdom of glory. He will reign with Christ for ever and ever (II Tim. 2: 12; Rom. 8: 17; Rev. 22: 5).

Thus the more faithfully a member of the "church of the firstborn" has responded to his spiritual birthright here on earth, the richer and more embracing will be his enjoyment of his heavenly birthright in eternity.

The heavenly prize will not be granted to the self-confident and self-satisfied but only to those who are striving and pressing on. Not every believer will attain to the *full* prize of the high calling of God in Christ Jesus. Least of all those who regard themselves as sure of it! Not in vain has the Lord said: "Blessed are they that hunger and thirst after righteousness: for they [they alone!] shall be filled" (Matt. 5: 6). In the original Greek the word "they" is emphasized strongly in order to show the exclusive nature of the promise. And Paul declares: "Know ye not that they which run in a race all run, but [only] one receiveth the prize? Even so *run*, that ye may attain" (I Cor. 9: 24). "And if a man also contend in the games, yet is he not crowned, except he have contended lawfully" (II Tim. 2: 5). Woe to the self-assured, self-approving ones! A great disappointment awaits them (I John 2: 28). But blessed are those that hunger and thirst! Blessed are the "imperfect" ones, *i.e.*, those who are conscious of their imperfections and therefore press on in the Lord's power: for *they* will attain the goal.

In all this there rules this encouraging fact:

The heavenly prize is not to be won by human and earthly endeavours but only by the power which grace gives to faith. All our own efforts are impotent and worthless. Even our very best ideals and strivings will not carry us through to the goal. Christ alone is able to do this. Therefore the runner in the race looks unto Him from whom all power comes. Every victory over sin, all growth in holiness, all progress in the race is entirely a gift of His free grace. There is no human merit at all. Only he who lives by the gifts of God's grace will be able to reach the goal in full triumph.

And what will happen when the great day of the prize-giving shall have come? Before God only His own work counts. We ourselves have accomplished nothing. All has been given by Himself, and now, in addition to all this, upon us, the receivers of His free gifts, who of ourselves have deserved nothing, He bestows the everlasting crown of honour. That means: He pours out upon us His gifts at the goal for the simple reason that we have accepted in faith His gifts on the way. He showers His blessings upon us at the winning-post simply because we have allowed Him to give us His free blessings during the race. Therefore although conditioned by the devotion of the one to be crowned, the prize of the race, the full enjoyment of the heavenly Birthright, is an entirely unmerited gift of a freely giving and generous God of mercy. It is "reward" out of "grace." Rightly did Tauler, the great German mediæval mystic (about 1400), say that when at last God gives the crowns, He is not going to crown us but to crown Christ in us, for only Christ is worthy of a crown.

In the Tower of London there is a wonderful treasure. Nowhere in the world is there a place where so many precious stones, jewels, and gold are stored together in such a small place as in that subterranean vault of the Wakefield Tower. We refer to the crown jewels of the British Empire. Swords, crowns, pearls, golden vessels of fabulous worth are exhibited here, illuminated most beautifully. Diamonds and precious stones sparkle in glittering light. There, for example, one sees the golden spoon, more than 700 years old, always used for the anointing of the British Kings and Queens. The sceptre of the British Empire with its golden cross, studded with jewels, with its chief ornament, the "Star of Africa," the largest diamond yet known in the whole world. I saw crowns of Queens, covered with hundreds and hundreds of precious stones and pearls. Further, there was the crown which King George wore in Delhi (India), and which, according to the official description, is ornamented with no less that 6,170 diamonds, emeralds, and sapphires. The most precious object of all is the Imperial State Crown, covered with radiant jewels of indescribable value, especially the world-renowned Cullinan Diamond. Almost 3,000 diamonds and hundreds of pearls and sapphires and rosary diamonds adorn it.

But what are all these crowns and the crowns of other nations in comparison to those crowns which Christ has to bestow? The "crown of righteousness" (II Tim. 4: 8), "the crown of life" (Rev. 2: 10), "the crown of rejoicing" (I Thess. 2: 19), "the incorruptible crown" (I Cor. 9: 25, 26), "the crown of glory" (I Pet. 5: 3, 4)? How much does all that is earthly pale before the glory of the heavenly! Even the highest earthly riches and beauties sink into absolute insignificance when compared with the Eternal and Divine ! In fact, not only the sufferings but also the glories of this world are not worthy even to be compared to the glories which shall be revealed in us (Rom. 8: 18).

Wreaths of olive branches and laurels, palms and festive garbs, were presented to the victorious runners in the Greek races. Christ, however, gives those who have served Him in faithfulness, the *heavenly* crown of honour.

Laurels, olive branches and palms wither away. Crowns sink down. But the crown of honour which Christ gives the victor will remain in everlasting life, with the freshness and flower of youth. Here is an incorruptible *possession* (I Pet. 1: 4), a *priesthood* eternally worshipping, a *royal dignity and rule* for all time and eternity (Rev. 22: 5). Thus the threefold privilege of the Birthright of the firstborn as richness, priesthood, and kingship, the prize for the overcomer, will remain for ever and ever.

All this will be ours if we look unto Jesus, and *run*.

As the "Firstborn from the dead" Christ is the great Victor over that greatest, combined, and most powerful enemy, sin, death, Satan. Thus He is altogether *the* Pioneer and decisive Conqueror in all situations. He Who was the Winner in the mightiest battle is certainly also able to gain the victory in all smaller ones. He can master every difficulty and can throw back every attack of the adversary. In any and every battle He can give practical victory and so bring us through to the final triumph.

As the "Firstborn among many brethren" He enables His own to share His glory in heaven (Rev. 3: 21; John 17: 22) and to attain the full blessing of the birthright, appointed to the first-born ones, the "firstfruits of His creatures" (James 1: 18). He Who after His own victorious battle has reached the goal triumphantly and is crowned with glory and honour (Heb. 2: 9), gives to every overcomer in the race the crown of rejoicing and honour.

Therefore ever anew, while running in the racecourse in the arena of faith,

"Let us look unto Jesus!"

CHAPTER VIII

LISTEN! GOD SPEAKS!

"For ye are not come unto a mount that might be touched, and that burned with fire, and unto blackness, and darkness, and tempest, and the sound of a trumpet, and the voice of words: which voice they that heard intreated that no word more should be spoken unto them: for they could not endure that which was enjoined, If even a beast touch the mountain, it shall be stoned; and so fearful was the appearance, that Moses said, I exceedingly fear and quake (Deut. 9: 19):

"But ye are come unto mount Zion, and unto the city of the living God, the heavenly Jerusalem, and to innumerable hosts of angels, to the general assembly and church of the firstborn who are enrolled in heaven, and to God the Judge of all, and to the spirits of just men made perfect, and to Jesus the mediator of a new covenant, and to the blood of sprinkling that speaketh better than that of Abel.

"See that ye refuse not him that speaketh. For if they escaped not, when they refused him that warned them on earth, much more shall not we escape, who turn away from him that warneth from heaven: whose voice then shook the earth: but now he hath promised, saying, Yet once more will I make to tremble not the earth only, but also the heaven. And this word, Yet once more, signifieth the removing of those things that are shaken, as of things that have been made, that those things which are not shaken may remain.

"Wherefore receiving a kingdom that cannot be shaken, let us have grace, whereby we may offer service well-pleasing to God with reverence and awe: for our God is a consuming fire" (Heb. 12: 18–29).

WHEN God speaks man must hearken. Each time God's word is preached we are personally addressed by Him. Then always our small self is directly confronted by His great Divine Self, and every such time is an hour of decision. A decision is made whether we mean to hearken or not, to obey

God or ignore Him, to harden ourselves or recognize in practice His claim and redeeming authority over us.

Most imposing and grand is the introduction to the second part of the book of Isaiah, this greatest prophet of the Old Testament, this bold "evangelist of the Old Covenant."

"The *voice* of one that crieth" (Isa. 40: 3).

"The *voice* of one saying" (Isa. 40: 6).

"Lift up thy *voice* with strength" (Isa. 40: 9).

Say:

"*Behold,* your God" (Isa. 40: 9).

"*Behold,* the Lord God will come" (Isa. 40: 10).

"*Behold,* His reward is with Him" (Isa. 40: 10).

Let us note:

Thrice: "Voice, voice, voice!"

Thrice: "Behold, behold, behold!"

These words strike our spiritual ear like six mighty blasts of a trumpet.

Listen! There is something you must *hear*! Pay attention! Let us *hearken*!

Look! There is something to be *seen*. Watch carefully! Let us *observe*!

Or, as it is written in the seven Letters to the churches in the book of the *Revelation*: "He that hath an ear, let him hear what the Spirit saith to the churches" (Rev. 2 and 3). This means: whosoever possesses any ability to perceive the things of God in his heart, whosoever possesses a spiritual organ to receive God's word in his soul, must now hearken. Whosoever, indeed, has a "receiving station" in his spiritual life for the "waves" from eternity, must hearken. Therefore again: When God speaks, man must listen. He must acknowledge that it involves an hour of decision.

This is the special message of the final section of Hebrews 12. "See that ye refuse not Him that speaketh" (Heb. 12: 25).

"Let us look unto Jesus." Let us *hearken* unto Him!

Four impressive reasons strengthen this command. They stand there like four shining golden exclamation marks to emphasize this New Testament warning and exhortation. One cannot avoid hearing and seeing them. At the same time the holy text looks back into the Old Testament and draws the conclusion: If in those earlier times the people were required to listen, how much more reason have we to listen to God's voice now! If the Old Testament saints, who lived in the introductory times of the preparation of salvation, were bound to hearken and to exercise practical obedience in faith, how much more *we* who live today in the times of the New Testament fulfilment! It is just this connexion and comparison between our being called "today" and God's call in the redemptive history of "yesterday" which makes this New Testament command so impressive and powerful: "Hearken, God speaketh."

First of all, however, the Scripture brings before us the riches of salvation which believers possess and for which they are held responsible before God.

I. *The Heavenly Riches of the Church of God*

Three marvellous facts shine forth before our vision with ever-increasing brilliance.

1. *As believers we have become spiritual possessors.* The letter to the Hebrews says: "Ye *are* come unto Mount Zion" (Heb. 12: 22). It is a perfect tense that is used (Gk. *proselelythate*). Thus something of vital importance has already happened. There is already an actual fact. A position of grace *is* occupied. A place of firm standing *has* been reached. You have already received something. It is a position at the foot of the heavenly mount of God. Even though the climbing to and reaching of the summit will not be completed before we get to glory, yet this present position, firmly connected with eternity, has already been given to us by grace as the basis and starting-point for our future exaltation.

It has been rightly said that believers are the only class of persons in the world who really *possess* anything. For all earthly "possessions" are only lent to us. At best we may be allowed to make use of them until the end of our life. But then we are forced to forsake every earthly property, and we shall leave this world just as empty as we came into it.

Furthermore: even *during* this limited period of time in which we can use earthly things, these never become bound up inextricably with the essence of our inward man. Possessor and possession remain always distinct and separate: they confront each other as subject and object, but they never become one. No earthly goods become organically or spiritually bound up with the central essence of man's personality. For this reason Jason calls all earthly property "foreign" things, *i.e.* they do not really enter into our soul, they do not become one with our spiritual essence and its deepest interests, and therefore are not really "our own" (Luke 16: 12), but belong, so to speak, to "another." The relationship never reaches oneness but always remains that of a duality.

But heavenly goods enter into our very nature. Therefore we have not only "received" light but we "are" become light (Eph. 5: 8). We have not only "been given" righteousness but "are" righteousness in Him (II Cor. 5: 21). The heavenly possession of salvation has been personally and organically grafted into us by Christ through the Holy Spirit. In this sense real believers are truly possessors.

2. *As possessors of spiritual blessings we have already received heavenly goods of the coming world.* We have come to "Mount Zion," the "city of the living God," the "heavenly Jerusalem," to "innumerable hosts of angels, the general assembly," which is living in eternity (Heb. 12: 22, 23). We *have* already arrived in principle where in full reality we shall be for ever. The future is already the present. In today we possess tomorrow. On earth we own heaven. We have been translated into the "heavenly places" with Christ (Eph. 2: 6). We have not only been crucified with Him, buried, and raised again with Him (Rom. 6: 3–6), but through the Holy Spirit we have spiritually experienced His ascension in our union with Him. Eternal life belongs to us in the very midst of time (John 3: 16, 36; 5: 24).

The expression "heavenly places" occurs only in the Ephesian letter, where it is used five times. Literally the original Greek says only, "in the heavenlies." So one has sought to supplement this expression by translating "heavenly *goods*" or "heavenly *blessings*" or "heavenly *kingdom*," especially in Eph. 1: 3. But the other contexts in which this expression appears, show quite clearly that it has a definite reference to the idea of "region, sphere, place," in, as it were, a certain "local" sense. In the same Ephesian letter Paul, using exactly the same expression (Gk. *en tois epouraniois*), says that God has "set Christ at His right hand in the heavenlies," which can only mean "in the heavenly *places*" (Eph. 1: 20). And in Ephesians 2: 6 he writes that God "raised us up with Him and made us to sit with Him in the heavenlies in Christ Jesus." Similarly, this can mean only, "in the heavenly *places*." In the third chapter of the same epistle the apostle speaks of "the principalities and the powers in the heavenlies" who are to recognize the wisdom of God in the church (v. 10), and in chapter 6 he mentions the "spiritual hosts of wickedness in the heavenlies" against whom we wrestle. All these Scriptures allow of only one interpretation, namely "heavenly places, regions, or spheres."

The impressive thought which lies at the bottom of all this is that the Christian by his new birth has been born into a heavenly life. His citizenship is in heaven. His entire life is conditioned by heaven. His joy is of a heavenly nature. His life's aim is heaven itself (Phil. 3: 20). Just as Christ, the last Adam, is "the Heavenly One" so we, being members of His body which is the new mankind, are also "the heavenly ones" (I Cor. 15: 48).

Thus the Christian, as long as he is on earth, lives in two worlds. He belongs to heaven and to earth simultaneously. Therein lies his nobility. Therein lies also the tension of his life. He knows that Christ his Redeemer, as the exalted One, is in heaven (Phil. 2: 9; Eph. 4: 10), and yet is indwelling him here on earth (Eph. 3: 17). And he himself, the redeemed one, is still living here on earth (John 17: 11), and yet he is translated with Christ to the heavenlies (Eph. 2: 6).

The living connexion between these two sides of the Christian standing is the Holy Spirit. For the Spirit came down from the risen "Christ *above* us," from heaven to earth (Acts 2: 33), and the Spirit, as the "Christ *in* us," leads us up from earth to heaven (Col. 1: 27; II Cor. 3: 17, 18).

Only on this foundation is it possible to be practically heavenly-minded. As long as the believer does not understand his heavenly position in Christ, he will always vacillate between *worldliness* and *legality*. For either he will neglect his fellowship with the Lord and his connexion with the heavenly world and allow himself to be captivated by earthly things, seeking and setting his mind on that which is *below*, or he will endeavour in his own strength to hold on to the heavenly *above*, but in a legal, slavish, joyless manner. It must result that he will never reach a really victorious life, simply for want of clear look of faith and spiritual understanding as to his position in grace and the heavenly resources which are at his disposal. What we need is a thankful recognition of the free grace given us in Christ, a practical acknowledgment of our heavenly standing, a trustful laying hold of the gifts of God in an attitude of devotion of heart and life. Thus a true heavenly-mindedness will inspire all areas of our life and permeate them in all directions and relationships.

Therefore give thanks for the redemption already received.   If sin assails you do not first *ask* for victory but at once thank the Lord that He *has* made you free from the slavery of sin.   When Jehoshaphat went to war against the Moabites and the Ammonites, *before* the commencement of the battle he ordered the singers and the harpers to praise the Lord in holy adornment, and the Lord gave His people the victory (II Chron. 20: 21, 22).   Thus joy in the Lord will be also our strength.

And still more:

3.   *As possessors of blessings of the coming eternal world—within this sphere of the heavenly—we have been set in association not just with some high level of this eternity, but even with its most important, indeed, its central and supreme regions and persons.*   Sevenfold is the description of the Old Testament Mount Sinai, as given in Heb. 12.   Those Israelitish hearers had come

to a mountain that might be touched,
to burning fire,
to blackness,
to thick darkness,
to tempest,
to the sound of a trumpet,
to the voice of words, which voice they that heard could not endure (Heb. 12: 18–20).

Eightfold is the description of the New Testament heavenly heights of salvation.   Ye are come
to Mount Zion,
to the city of the living God, the heavenly Jerusalem,
to innumerable hosts of angels, the general assembly,
to the church of the firstborn who are enrolled in heaven,
to God, the Judge of all,
to the spirits of just men made perfect,
    and further:
to Jesus, the Mediator of a New Covenant,
to the blood of sprinkling that speaketh better than that of Abel (Heb. 12: 22–24).

Two groups of heavenly realities can be clearly distinguished here.   The first group comprises six, and the second group the last two members of this golden chain.

Transcendancy and heavenly nature characterize the first

group, and grace the second. Glory is predominant in the former and salvation in the latter.

The first contains something twofold: we have been brought to the most central heavenly *regions*: Mount Zion, the city of the living God, the heavenly Jerusalem: and

to the most glorious of spiritually glorified *beings*, that is to persons who either live themselves in heaven, or in the region of heavenly blessings, namely to God, the Judge of all, the angels innumerable, the firstborn who are enrolled in heaven, the spirits of just men made perfect.

That in the midst of the description of New Testament glories God is called "the judge of all" does not mean that, in spite of our salvation there is after all to be faced something terrible which may rob us of all our joy, as if finally everything were still uncertain and God as our judge might possibly some day condemn us: no, it means that the great gift of the gospel is precisely this, that we are already reconciled with the Judge, that we can come into His presence without fear and live in His good pleasure. The great community of which we are citizens is ruled over by righteousness. Its head is the Divine Judge who puts away all injustice, who helps and liberates the oppressed, and who gives everyone his due position and gift according to His own Holy Divine order of justice.

Some expositors suggest that, in addition to this, a still greater and far higher blessing is expressed here. The phrase "ye have come" which introduces the eight blessings, enumerated in connexion with this golden chain of heavenly persons, realities and blessings, has, in all the seven other cases quite apparently the meaning "ye are come *to share in* these dignities mentioned." "Ye are come *to share in* the glory of the heavenly Jerusalem," "Ye are come *to share in* the blessings of the New Covenant," "Ye are come *to share in* the saving results of the blood of sprinkling that speaketh better than that of Abel." So, interpreting these clauses with uniformity, the following may be the sense of the statement, "ye are come to God the Judge of all"; "Ye are come to *share with Him* the honour of the office indicated by this title." Ye are come to share God's office as Judge. "The saints are to judge the world and even angels (I Cor. 6: 2, 3). The apostles are assured of this office in relation to Israel as a nation (Luke 22: 28–30). The same thought is suggested by the promise of sitting upon the throne with Christ, the Judge (Rev. 3: 21); that is, by the dignity of kingship being conferred, for of old the king was the chief judge of the people; and by such a promise as that to the saints who overcome, that they shall rule the nations (Rev. 2: 27). In the administration of His mighty kingdom, and in the adjusting and rewarding of the affairs of the ages of human and angelic history, the glorified saints will be associated with the King in glory" (G. H. Lang).

The "church of the firstborn who are enrolled in heaven" are obviously the believers living in the present dispensation here on earth. Also in all other Scriptures where the word "ecclesia" (church) refers to men only (only rarely it refers to angels, as in Psa. 89: 6), it signified the body of the redeemed as they are living in their present form of spiritual and organic fellowship of life and faith here on earth. It indicates the invisible heavenly side of the church, its eternal nobility which the church possesses already today while still living in this world and not yet in the world to come. The believers "are" not yet in heaven but they are already "enrolled" in heaven. By grace they have a right to heaven. Their *name*, although not yet their *person*, is already in heaven. They have their home-country in heaven, their citizen rights are in heaven, and their goal is heaven (Phil. 3: 20). They are *registered* in heaven. If it were meant to refer to any already living as perfected ones in heaven itself, the expression that their names are "written" in heaven would scarcely have been used. For this designation undoubtedly emphasizes the *contrast* between the high calling of the group of persons referred to here and their present lowly situation and the battle which they have yet to win on this earth.

In the same way Paul says of "fellow-labourers" in the gospel that "their names are in the book of life" (Phil. 4: 3), thus using this expression of contemporaries of his own life and time, and therefore of members of the church of Christ who still lived on *earth*. Likewise the Lord said to the Seventy whom He had sent out, and who then returned to Him full of joy after having done miracles and cast out evil spirits in His name: "Rejoice not that the spirits are subject unto you; but rejoice that your names are written in heaven" (Luke 10: 20). So also here this expression is used with regard to people who were living on *earth*, believing in Christ.

True believers belong in the reality of things to the ranks and regions which have as their centre the throne of God and of the Lamb (Gal. 4: 26; Eph. 2: 18). Although they are still on earth and dwell in the perishing tabernacle of this body, yet they are far less distant from the face of God, from the enjoyment of the treasures of His house, and from the fellowship of all those around Him, than the people of the Old Covenant were, when they were allowed to approach the mountain on which the glory of God appeared, but which they were forbidden to touch under penalty of death. Their "approaching" remained "a standing at a distance."

It is, however, the wonderful privilege of the New Testament salvation that faith gives us true access to and real, present entrance into God's world. Thus we are far closer to the heavenly Mount Zion which we *cannot* see, than the people of Israel were to the earthly Mount Sinai which they *could* see with their bodily eyes.

In connexion with this people of God living on earth, there are named also "the spirits of just men made perfect" (Heb. 12: 23). Thus the perfected ones in heaven are linked together with the church on earth. God's people "above" and God's people "below" are regarded as one unity. For God's kingdom links up heaven, paradise and earth, and past and present. Even death cannot dissolve and break the unity of the kingdom of God. Its "spaces" such as heaven, paradise and earth, and its "times" such as past and present, form one uniform organism which has harmony and unity embracing aeons and dispensations, time and eternity.

The last two links in our great golden chain of Heb. 12 speak of grace and salvation: of Jesus the Mediator of the New Covenant, of the blood of sprinkling which speaketh better than that of Abel. Thus the description of the heavenly Mount Zion ends by referring to the redemptive work of the Saviour, and *three most important mountains* rise before our spiritual vision:

the flaming, thundering Mount Sinai,

the radiant Mount Zion of the heavenly Jerusalem, and

the simple hill called Golgotha.

This, however, is the wonderful way of salvation: The work of the Saviour accomplished on the earthly *hill Golgotha* has brought all that believe into contact with the heavenly *Mount Zion*—excluding all the works connected with the Old Testament *Mount Sinai*.

Thus the whole riches of heaven stand before our vision:

the highest heavenly regions,

the most glorious heavenly persons,

the inexhaustible heavenly springs and resources of grace and salvation.

And all this has been opened up to us by the blood of Jesus our Substitute and Redeemer, His precious blood shed for our sakes on the cross of Calvary.

We are not intended to live only in heaven's "frontier provinces," so to speak, in the outer districts, in the suburbs of the heavenlies, but in the central royal castle of the Most High Himself, in His eternal city, in the heavenly Jerusalem: just as the residence and royal palace of King David stood at one time in the earthly Jerusalem on Mount Zion. It is God's will to join us to Himself. We are called to reign with Christ and to live in His heavenly Capital, in the city of the living God, in the centre of the super-cosmos, in the glorious metropolis of the transcendent world of Eternity. For this reason Christ will write the name of the city of His God on the foreheads of the overcomers, "the name of my God and the name of the city of my God, the new Jerusalem, which cometh down out of heaven from my God" (Rev. 3: 12). Paul declares: "The Jerusalem that is above is free, which is our mother" (Gal. 4: 26).

How could we attain all this if the blood of the Son of God had not flowed, the "blood of sprinkling which speaketh better than that of Abel," the blood by means of which He has become "the Mediator of a new covenant"? The blood of Abel cried for vengeance (Gen. 4: 10), the blood of Jesus for grace.

> Heaven is open, my soul, oh knowest thou why?
> Because Jesus, thy Saviour, once bled and did die.

The well-known preacher of the gospel, Charles Haddon Spurgeon, who for many decades preached Sunday by Sunday the message of salvation to thousands of hearers in his vast Tabernacle in London, was undoubtedly one of the most gifted and most learned among God's servants. Spiritually and intellectually his person and ministry stood out in a most remarkable and unique manner. What, however, was his confession at the end of his blessed life? When he lay upon his death-bed, after so many years of fruitful service, he said to his friends who visited him: "My brethren, my theology has become very simple. It consists of four words:

> *"Jesus died for me."*

This, indeed, will be truly the confession of all real believers:

"Jesus died for me." This will be the main melody in all the hymns of thanks of all the redeemed in the heavenly glory. Unto all the aeons of eternity the main theme of all worship and praise on the *heavenly* Mount Zion will be the suffering and work of the Saviour accomplished on the *earthly* "Mount" Golgotha. "And I heard a voice of many angels round about the throne and the living creatures and the elders: and the number of them was ten thousand times ten thousand, and thousands of thousands; saying with a great voice, Worthy is the Lamb that hath been slain to receive the power, and riches, and wisdom, and might, and honour, and glory, and blessing" (Rev. 5: 11, 12).

But all this is only *one* side of the truth considered. To emphasize the present and the coming, the spiritual and the eternal glories of God's salvation is actually not the *main* object of our Scripture when considered in the whole context of the passage (Heb. 12: 18–22). Although undoubtedly contained here and plainly expressed, it does not stand in the foreground of the holy text. Let us notice that this whole section of Scripture is introduced by the small word "for." "*For* ye are not come (unto the mount of the Old Testament) . . ., but ye are come unto (the heavenly mountain)." The whole is thus not an independent line of thought, complete in itself, but an argument of *reasoning.* As such it is subject to other main thoughts, the correctness and impressiveness of which it has to emphasize by this "for," which introduces the following words as an establishment of proofs. This main line of thought is, in the clear context of our passage, the command to practical holiness: "Wherefore lift up the hands that hang down, and the palsied knees. . . . Pursue [follow after] peace with all men, and the sanctification without which no man shall see the Lord. . . . FOR ye are not come unto" the Old Testament Mount Sinai of the law, but to the New Testament glorious Mountain of salvation. This is the leading idea.

It brings before our vision the main message of the final section of this chapter. The reference to the glorious standing of the redeemed in grace is used to underline the seriousness of their personal responsibility. Just *because* we have become so rich in Christ and *because* the eternal prize is so glorious, therefore practical, complete devotion is required of us. Just *because* a heavenly goal is offered by the Divine Umpire, the runner in the "arena of faith" has to press on.

M

II.   The Holy Obligations of those Called to Heavenly Glory

Here too we can recognize three aspects.

1.   *Riches involve obligations.   "Noblesse oblige."*   For the very
reason that we have received so much blessing from God, all the
more devotion and sanctification are expected of us.   In ordinary
earthly life debts usually arise from poverty; in spiritual life,
however, our "debts" arise out of our *riches!*   Paul declares in
Romans: "I am a debtor" (Rom. 1: 14).   He is speaking there
of his personal missionary commission; but the principle remains
valid in general.   Because we *possess* the message of salvation,
we are "indebted" to pass it on to others.   Because we *possess*
the fulness of blessing, we are "indebted" to live in the power
of spiritual victory.   Because we have become kings we are
"indebted" to live up practically to our high royal standing.
Nobles must conduct themselves nobly.   He who intends to
reach the goal must behave himself according to the nature and
character of this goal.   Because we are appointed to heaven and
glory, we must live on earth "worthily" of our glorious heavenly
calling (Eph. 4: 1).

The greater the riches, the more comprehensive the obligations.   The more bountiful the gifts of grace, the more serious
the responsibility of the receiver.   "To whomsoever much is
given, of him shall much be required" (Luke 12: 48).

To emphasize this most serious demand the holy text shows us
four impressive reasons, comparing the Old Testament and New
Testament spiritual situations.

*Listen!   God speaks!   Pay the more attention!   For the New
Testament* STANDING IN SALVATION *is higher.*

If already the Old Testament saints had to be obedient, how
much more *we!*   If in those ancient times they had to listen to
the voice of Him that spoke to them, how much more should *we*
listen today!   Therefore: "See that ye refuse not him that
speaketh."   Now in our present time, in the New Testament
dispensation of salvation, attention and obedience are required to
such an extent as never before in the whole history of revelation.
In this obedience of faith the New Testament saints should excel
all preceding generations of believers in devotion and sanctification.

This is the meaning of the comparing and contrasting of Mount
Sinai to the heavenly Mount Zion in our passage.   Ye should
press on to sanctification, *"for"* ye are not come to the mountain

of the Law but to the heavenly mountain of Divine salvation and glory. Freedom from the law does not make men a law unto themselves, but all the more zealous and actively holy. It is the same as when Paul says: "Sin shall not have dominion over you: *for* (!) ye are not under law [Mount Sinai], but under grace [New Testament standing of salvation, the heavenly Mount Zion]" (Rom. 6: 14).

The New Testament revelation takes the fact that we are "under" grace in its full reality and weight. Grace is "above" us. Grace has become our ruler. Grace claims to govern "royally" (Rom. 5: 21. Gk. *basileuein, cf. basileus,* king). We have to be subject to grace, we have to obey her. Let us hearken to Jesus: He is our Lord!

But still more.

Listen! God speaks! Pay the more attention! For the PLATFORM OF THE NEW TESTAMENT DIVINE SPEAKER *is higher.*

Long ago God spoke from the height of an earthly mount; but now He speaks from heaven through Christ His Son, who has been exalted to the heavenly Divine Throne. The designation in the text of Mount Sinai as a mount which "might be touched" (Heb. 12: 18) is intended to characterize it as something outwardly perceptible and earthly. But Mount Zion, the city of the living God above, is, in contrast, something transcendental, super-sensible, and heavenly. God spoke to the Jews from a mountain which might be touched, which was earthly, and used as His interpreter an *earthly* man, Moses. In the New Covenant, however, He speaks from *heaven,* using as interpreter His only begotten Son, whom He had sent down from heaven to accomplish the redemptive work, and who, having been exalted again by His Father to heaven's glory, now speaks through His Spirit to His own (Heb. 1: 1).

This means at the same time a considerable increase of responsibility, compared to that of the Old Testament hearers. "For if they escaped not when they refused him that warned them on earth, much more shall not we escape who turn away from him that warneth from heaven" (Heb. 12: 25).

Undoubtedly *God* is the speaker also here. The holy text does not intend to point to a difference in the Divine *persons* who speak in the Old and New Testament revelations, but rather to a difference in the Divine *methods* of revelation. The speaking of "God" and the speaking of "Christ" are not to be fundamentally distinguished as separated from or opposed to each other. God speaks in Christ through the Holy Spirit. Each time God's Word is being preached, Christ "comes" to us through the Spirit of God (Eph. 2: 17).

We must be prepared to hear the Divine voice as speaking from heaven. Though perhaps sitting in an earthly meeting-room, chapel, or church building, and listening to the message delivered by God's servants, it is not the word of men which is being preached, nor mere Bible expositions, spiritual medita-tions, or Biblical thoughts *about* God's Word, but the very *Word of God itself*. That is the high nobility and at the same time the serious responsibility of every proclamation and preaching of the gospel. "If any man speaketh, speaking as it were oracles of God" (I Pet. 4: 11). "We thank God without ceasing, that, when ye received from us the word of the message, even the word of God, ye accepted it not as the word of man, but, as it is in truth, the word of God, which also worketh in you that believe" (I Thess. 2: 13). "As the Lord liveth, what my God saith, that will I speak" (II Chron. 18: 13). "Now therefore we are all here present in the sight of God, to hear all things that have been commanded thee of the Lord" (Acts 10: 33).

If, however, our oral proclamation of the Word has to be not merely a speaking "about" God's word, but "word of God" itself, it must contain the following spiritual characteristics:

the truth of the message of God,
the love of the heart of God,
the tact of the wisdom of God,
the leading of the Spirit of God,
the power of the authority of God, and above all and in all:
the presence of the Person of God in Christ through the Holy
    Spirit.

In the King's word is power. In *His* word alone! Not in the words of His servants, however experienced and sanctified they may be. What we need in increased measure is the holy con-sciousness that, as God's witnesses, we are at the same time God's *mouth*. What the world needs is not learned lectures, elegant speeches, homiletically well thought out, even though these may be valuable in due time and place, but a powerful, living witness which goes from heart to heart, kindled by the life of God and guided and empowered by the Holy Spirit. "Give the people bread; for they do not wish straw, nor do they eat flowers" (Prof. Warneck). Only thus our oral preaching and witnessing, private as well as public, will prove to be that which it ought to be. Then opening of doors in countries and among nations, the conversion of sinners, and the sanctification of believers will be more and more a living proof, renewed daily, of the truth and reliability of the Divine promise: "For as the rain cometh down and the snow from heaven, and returneth not thither, but watereth the earth, and maketh it bring forth and bud, and giveth seed to the sower and bread to the eater; so shall my word be that goeth forth out of my mouth: it shall not return unto me void, but it shall accomplish that which I please, and it shall prosper in the thing whereto I sent it" (Isa. 55: 10, 11).

And how manifold and all-inclusive is the speaking of the great God! He speaks through

the symbolic language of nature (Rom. 1: 19, 20; Psa. 19: 1–3);

the historical language of experience, both in national and individual life;

the inward language of man's conscience (Psa. 32: 3, 4; Rom. 2: 14, 15);

the personal language of His witnesses (II Cor. 5: 20);

the book language of the written Word, the Bible (II Tim. 3: 16);

the direct language in Christ the living Word (Heb. 1: 1; Eph. 2: 17);

and one day He will speak to men through

the legal language of the judgment to come (Psa. 2: 5).

Furthermore: The writer of *Hebrews* continues to prove the higher New Testament responsibility by comparing a third aspect of the Old Testament word with the New Testament.

Listen! God speaks! Pay the more attention! For the SPHERE OF ACTION *of the New Testament Divine Word is more comprehensive, indeed, is universal.*

In both cases certain effects upon nature and creation in general are connected with God's Word. In this the effects upon nature wrought by the Old Testament word of Mount Sinai were restricted to the *earth*—to fire and storm, darkness and thick blackness, earthquake and the voice of trumpets. But the effects upon nature to be brought about one day by the New Testament word of God, will extend into the *heavens*: "Yet once more will I make to tremble not the earth only, but also the heaven" (Heb. 12: 26).

And finally:

Listen! God speaks! Pay the more attention! For the EFFI-CACY *of the New Testament Divine Word is mightier.*

At Sinai the earth was only "shaken" (v. 26), but in the end-times heaven and earth will be "*changed*," "removed" by God's Word (Heb. 12: 27). "Changing" or "removing," however, is something more fundamental than only "shaking."

With these four chief arguments the holy text has given an overwhelming demonstration of the greater responsibility of the New Testament hearers in contrast to the receivers of the Old Testament revelation. These four points of view are

spiritually:

the New Testament standing of salvation is nobler;

Christologically:

the platform of the New Testament Divine Speaker is higher;

cosmologically:

the sphere of action of the New Testament Divine word is more comprehensive (heaven, not only earth);

eschatologically:

the efficacy of the New Testament Divine word is mightier (changing and perfecting of the world, not only shaking).

Therefore once more:

Listen! God speaks!

Men who are called to such heavenly destinies, who are to receive an eternal kingdom that cannot be shaken, who are addressed, through the Word and the Holy Spirit, by such an exalted Majesty as God Himself, whose voice comes from His own Throne of Glory, and thus from the Central Source of the universe, from the Holiest of Holies of Heaven and Eternity, such men must be heavenly-minded! According to God's will they have to be watching and waiting; with the pilgrim's staff in their hands, their lamps trimmed and shining, ready to go out to meet the Bridegroom (Luke 12: 35); men and women who regard "the last things" as the "first" and who wait for the returning Lord, who "always live in the eleventh hour of the day" (Soren Kierkegaard). No doubt they will perform their earthly duties conscientiously and with care, and yet their real goal is heaven. On earth they are examples of correctness, faithfulness, relia-bility; but joyfully they look forward to the revelation of the kingdom of God. They know: "Our citizenship is in heaven; from whence also we wait for a Saviour, the Lord Jesus Christ; who shall fashion anew the body of our humiliation, that it may be conformed to the body of his glory" (Phil. 3: 20, 21).

Therefore: "Gird up the loins of your mind, be sober, and set your hope perfectly on the grace that is to be brought unto you

at the revelation of Jesus Christ" (I Pet. 1: 13). Our attitude of
mind should be that of a man who has girded up his loose, wide,
outer garment with his belt, so as to be better able to stride forward unhindered. That means that our attitude of mind should
be purposeful. In holy concentration we should aim at the one
thing necessary—eternity. Our attitude should be steadfast, not
wavering, light-hearted, distracted. We must press forward in
Spirit-wrought energy of will, just as Paul, the great servant
of Christ, declares of his own striving and pressing on: "Forgetting the things which are behind and stretching forward to
the things which are before, I press on toward the goal unto the
prize of the high calling of God in Christ Jesus. Let us therefore, as many as be perfect [full-grown], be thus minded" (Phil.
3: 13–15).

In all this, however, it is not simply left to our own choice
whether or not we are inclined to press on in the arena of faith,
to obey or disobey the Lord. No, great and weighty consequences are bound up with our decision. We are placed
before an unavoidable alternative—whether we will rise up
towards heaven, or sink down, whether we will win or lose,
become established or be shaken. This is the fundamental law
of all spiritual life. It flourishes only when in practical contact
with its Divine source. In ourselves there is no guarantee of
anything. The guarantee for our being kept and perfected lies
in Christ alone. Therefore everything is dependent upon our
constant life-fellowship with Him, every step forward and every
victory, all progress in spiritual growth.

2. *Riches present no mechanical guarantees.* You may have
begun in spiritual blessing and may now live in misery and
poverty. You may have had sunny times of joy in Christ, and of
victory, and yet now be lying down in defeat and dark depression.

Just this is the historical background of our passage in Hebrews. Only for this reason was the whole Hebrews letter
written. Therefore take this message earnestly to heart and
conscience: Riches present no undisputed guarantees! In spite
of most blessed beginnings we may get into spiritual decline and
impoverishment. In the past you may have borne witness to
Christ with courage and joy: today perhaps you are standing
back in cowardice. Formerly you may have loved your brethren and sisters; today you may have contention and strife with
them. In days gone by you may have read and received God's
word into your heart carefully: today it is a closed book to you.

Hitherto you may have been an "ornament" of the gospel, "adorning," as Paul says, the doctrine of God our Saviour (Titus 2: 10): today you are perhaps a stumbling-block for others, and your walk in life may "profane" the name of the Lord among men (cf. Ezek. 36: 22). Indeed, you may have left your "first love" (Rev. 2: 4).

But keep in mind: Blessed experiences of the past are no guarantees for equal fulness of blessings in the present and future. A Christ of only "yesterday" does not help you, but the living Christ of "today" always does. Our vision must not be directed only backwards—however fundamental our former experiences may be—but upwards and forwards. "It is not the beginning but the end that crowns the Christian's pilgrimage."

Thus, while fully enjoying the abundance of His grace, live in holy earnestness. These two things always belong together: certainty of salvation and the fear of God, joy and seriousness.

Joy without earnestness would become superficiality; earnestness without joy might develop into pessimism. Certainty of salvation without the fear of God becomes Pharisaism; fear of God without certainty of salvation tends to legalism and slavish anxiety. In reality, however, each of these characteristics is only present, in its God-intended spiritual sense, when the other is also present. Either we bear both in our hearts or none. And the measure of the one determines the measure of the other.

It is an alarming fact that in many Christian circles, whatever their name, holy reverence among believers is to a large extent lacking. General chattering about everyday matters precedes and follows many services. Not seldom spiritual hymns are sung thoughtlessly and mechanically without real attention to their contents. Sometimes, while singing, one is not even conscious that the hymn is a prayer to God. And sometimes there is a danger that even the ministry of the Word is presented in an irreverent way, as a self-pleasing talk "about" God's word, instead of being a holy proclamation of God's Word itself, delivered with the consciousness of responsibility, and Spirit-wrought, earnest, prayerful, in the authority of the Holy Ghost.

And how often, at the end of the service there come the "fowls of the air," in the form of superficial conversations, talks about business or politics, discussions about family matters and everyday life, and these steal away the seed which had been sown in the hearts? (Matt. 13: 4, 19).

How can this be helped? What can be the remedy?

Only a renewed listening to God, a fresh recognition of the authority of His commands, a restored conscious devotion and dedication of our hearts and lives to Him.

"Let us look unto Jesus!"

Let us hearken to His word.

Thus shall we receive at the same time new commissions from the Lord. New life and activity will enter our life. We shall learn to regard the riches of salvation which we have received from the Lord as a heavenly capital which has been deposited in our life and with which we have to trade for Him.

3. *Riches must be realized.* "*Therefore* receiving a kingdom that cannot be shaken, let us have grace, whereby we may offer ₊service well-pleasing to God with reverence and awe (godly fear)" (Heb. 12: 28). This "therefore" emphasizes the practical consequence.

The Greek word for "grace" (Gk. *charis*) means in addition "thanks." There are passages in which both translations of the word fit. Thus in this Scripture also.

The fundamental root meaning of the word is "something which gives joy." The root of *charis* is related to the Greek *chara*, joy (*cf. chairein*, to rejoice), and since for the Greek scarcely anything brought greater joy than beauty, the word received the meaning "graciousness, loveliness," *e.g.*, Luke 4: 22; Eph. 4: 29. From this its root meaning its application was extended to designating the attitude of a man who causes joy, that is "benevolence, favourable inclination," especially in the case of persons in high positions, *i.e.*, high officials, mostly kings. And as the oriental ruler had an unrestricted power and sovereignty, such an expression of his favour, which proceeded from his own free will alone, was at the same time an *un*earned gift, that is "grace," an *un*deserved present which brought with it fulness, glory, joy, and exaltation for the receiver. Since, however, the normal reaction to such unmerited liberality of the giver is the thankfulness of the receiver, the word "favourableness" received also the meaning of "gratitude." Thus on the one side it expresses the favourable inclination of the giver to the receiver, and on the other side the confession of the favourable inclination of the receiver to the giver.

This usage of the word is deeply significant. Therefore in the New Testament the word for "grace" is the same as for "thanks." To thank means: "to look up from the gift to the giver, to rejoice in his goodness, and to devote oneself to him with the sentiments of one's heart and with the deeds of one's life."

In this sense *both* meanings are true:

Since we have received a kingdom which cannot be shaken, we desire to prove ourselves *thankful* and to serve Him in sincerity and reverence who has given us His gifts and who is still blessing us so abundantly. Therefore, "Let us have thankfulness!" (R.V. footnote), And:

Since we have received such a kingdom, we long to live wholly for Him and to glorify His name, but we know that we can do this only in His own strength, in the power which His *grace* bestows upon us. Therefore: "Let us have grace!" (A. and R.V.)

Thus joyful sanctification results. All is sunshine. Grace is radiant *above* us, and gratitude is like an atmosphere of light *in* us. Grace descends from above; gratefulness ascends from below. He who really has understood grace, cannot be but grateful. He who is grateful receives grace ever anew.

Thus sanctification and joy go together. Lack of sanctification clouds real joy; true Spirit-filled joy, however, lends wings to sanctification.

Ungrateful Christians receive no new blessings. Although the Lord is a generous and willing giver, the measure of our actually being blessed is dependent upon our practical gratefulness and devotion.

How foolish therefore to lament and groan instead of rejoicing in God's goodness. By worrying we are robbing ourselves. Unthankfulness leads to spiritual poverty. But our whole life should be a constant practical thank-offering full of joy.

And how impressive is the whole context in which the Spirit of God has placed this, His exhortation. He begins the description of the riches of the New Testament by pointing to heaven and glory, and He finishes it by referring to judgment: "for our God is a consuming fire!" *God's grace at the beginning, God's flaming zeal at the end, and in the middle the exhortation: "Listen! God speaks!"* The words "heavenly Jerusalem" (v. 22) and "consuming fire" (v. 29) enclose this impressive command like a frame.

All this is written by a co-worker of the apostle Paul (*cf.* Heb. 13: 23), that is, of the apostle of free grace (!). It is written to Jewish Christian believers in the dispensation of the church. In the church, however, there is no difference in principle between the believers from Israel and the believers from the nations as to their standing in Christ. This has been repeatedly expressed in the teachings of Paul. So also we as Gentile Christians have to apply to ourselves the spiritual message of the letter to the Hebrews (Eph. 2: 13–22; 3: 6; Acts 28: 28; *cf.* Acts 10: 47; 11: 17; 15: 9–11).

Therefore let us not blunt the edge of this warning! Let us accept the Divine word in its full weight! We do not believe that our Scripture teaches the possibility of a believer being eternally lost in case of his personal, practical failure. But on the other hand, we as believers have to face most serious consequences if we are unfaithful and disobedient.

Therefore away with all fleshly religious self-security! The truth of the eternal salvation of the regenerate must never be made a soft pillow for superficiality and self-sufficiency. It is true that those who believe in Christ have passed from death to life; but as to the standard and measure of their glorification the following principle and exhortation is valid: "Give diligence to make your calling and election sure" (II Pet. 1: 10). "Follow after the sanctification, without which no man shall see the Lord" (Heb. 12: 14). "Let him that thinketh he standeth take heed lest he fall" (I Cor. 10: 12). What we need is a permanent attitude of faith, a continual, practical "Yes" to the Lord, which at the same time means an actual "No" to sin, a living, practical fellowship with Christ as the Crucified and Risen One. "Reckon ye also yourselves to be dead unto sin, but alive unto God in Christ Jesus" (Rom. 6: 11).

There is full salvation in Christ. In Him is life and victory. His word is not only commandment but is at the same time a creative source of strength. It is order and gift, precept and promise, commission and equipment.

To preach Him, this Redeemer, to mankind is our task under the New Covenant. He Himself is the essential contents of God's Word (II Cor. 4: 5). He is the Victor, the Truth in Person, the Salvation of the world. He lightens up the souls of those who are perishing in darkness. He stills their longings, quickens their hearts, frees them from sins, makes them holy and pure. Through Him they have recovered the lost Paradise. Their past is ordered, their present is illuminated, and their future is secured. Therefore God says: "Behold, my servant, whom I uphold, my chosen in whom my soul delighteth; I the Lord have called thee in righteousness . . . and given thee for a covenant of the people, for a light of the Gentiles" (Isa. 42: 1, 6). And in New Testament times the Father declared at the transfiguration of the Incarnate on the holy mountain, "This is My beloved Son, in whom I am well pleased."

"*Hear ye Him!*" (Matt. 17: 5).

"LET US LOOK UNTO JESUS!"